Dear Chandler, Dear Scarlett

Mike Huckabee

Dear Chandler,
Dear Scarlett

A Grandfather's Thoughts
on Faith, Family,
and the Things That
Matter Most

SENTINEL

SENTINEL
Published by the Penguin Group
Penguin Group (USA) Inc., 375 Hudson Street, New York, New York 10014, U.S.A.
Penguin Group (Canada), 90 Eglinton Avenue East, Suite 700, Toronto, Ontario,
Canada M4P 2Y3 (a division of Pearson Penguin Canada Inc.)
Penguin Books Ltd, 80 Strand, London WC2R 0RL, England
Penguin Ireland, 25 St. Stephen's Green, Dublin 2, Ireland (a division of Penguin Books Ltd)
Penguin Group (Australia), 707 Collins Street, Melbourne, Victoria 3008 Australia
(a division of Pearson Australia Group Pty Ltd)
Penguin Books India Pvt Ltd, 11 Community Centre, Panchsheel Park, New Delhi – 110 017, India
Penguin Group (NZ), 67 Apollo Drive, Rosedale, Auckland 0632, New Zealand
(a division of Pearson New Zealand Ltd)
Penguin Books, Rosebank Office Park, 181 Jan Smuts Avenue, Parktown North 2193, South Africa
Penguin China, B7 Jaiming Center, 27 East Third Ring Road North,
Chaoyang District, Beijing 100020, China

Penguin Books Ltd, Registered Offices: 80 Strand, London WC2R 0RL, England

First published in 2012 by Sentinel, a member of Penguin Group (USA) Inc.

1 3 5 7 9 10 8 6 4 2

Copyright © Mike Huckabee, 2012   All rights reserved

Illustrations by Debra Tilley

LIBRARY OF CONGRESS CATALOGING-IN-PUBLICATION DATA
Huckabee, Mike, 1955–
Dear Chandler, Dear Scarlett : a grandfather's thoughts on faith, family,
and the things that matter most / Mike Huckabee.
p. cm.
ISBN 978-1-59523-093-5
1. Children—Religious life. 2. Children—Conduct of life. 3. Grandparent and
child—Religious aspects—Christianity. 4. Grandfathers—Religious life. I. Title.
BV4571.3.H83 2012   248.4—dc23   2012027036

Printed in the United States of America · Set in Gazette LT Std · Designed by Amy Hill

ALWAYS LEARNING   PEARSON

I'm blessed with a wonderful wife of almost thirty-nine years; three grown children who have been the joy of my life (I've watched their births, their growth into adults, and their launching forth on their on); and three dogs, which make me laugh and keep me company when no one else is willing to stay up late or get up early. But this book is actually dedicated to the two members of my family who have become as much a part of me as the wife, kids, and dogs—and to be named up there with the dogs is really a big deal!

I dedicate this book to Chandler's mother, my daughter-in-law, Lauren, and to Scarlett's father, my son-in-law, Bryan Sanders. If marriages were still "arranged" as in ancient days, I could have only hoped to find Lauren and Bryan as spouses for my two married children. Their devotion as spouses to my children is rivaled only by their total immersion into the enormous responsibilities of parenthood. I hope and pray David and Sarah realize how blessed they truly are to have joined themselves to partners who love God, their families, and their country. The fact that Lauren and Bryan are delightful parents to my grandchildren certainly sweetens the pot! I love them as if they were my own. In gratitude to God, I dedicate this book to Lauren and Bryan.

too (he'd better, if he wanted to get paid!), and I'd be broadcasting her photo to my TV viewers each week.

Becoming a grandparent has been life changing, but beyond the sheer joy of it all, there is some very real responsibility that has weighed heavily on me. Like every grandparent, I hope to give even better counsel than I did with my own kids. After all, when I was raising them, I was a total neophyte at being a parent and had to learn everything as I went along. Now, many years, and many gray hairs, later, I have the perspective that comes with having taken the whole job of parenting from concept to completion, so to speak. I'm sure their parents are terrified I'll mess their kids up the way they think I messed them up, but, hey, they turned out okay!

And besides, Chandler's and Scarlett's parents are going to be very busy just keeping the kids fed and clothed and getting them to soccer practice and Scouts (sweet revenge for when I had to do all those things thirty years ago). Someone has to take charge of the big stuff. Of course, like any proud grandpa, I intend to spoil my grandkids rotten whenever they come to visit, but I also want to offer them something of greater value than my collection of vintage guitars, firearms (if Scarlett is anything like her mother, she won't find these very useful anyway), and photos of me hanging out with far more famous and important people from my days in politics or media. I want to give them something that won't collect dust and can't be auctioned on eBay. They are my blood-kin descendants, but I want them to inherit more from me than whatever I put in my will. I want to give them my wisdom and teach them the lessons I've learned in my fifty-seven years on this earth. Do I expect them to heed all of my advice and cling to every word? Not really. They probably won't understand most of it until they are about sixteen, and at that point, well, if they're like all other teenagers, I can't imagine they'll be looking for advice from their elders and trying to identify *more* with their relatives. But maybe one day Chandler and Scarlett will remember and understand the things I tell them.

Although my advice comes from my personal experience and I'm writing with my grandkids in mind, I hope any parent, grandparent, child, or grandchild can take away something valuable from these letters. I'll try not to be too obnoxious, but, don't worry, if you ever sit next to me on a plane, I'll still be happy to show you all the photos I have on my phone.

Dear Chandler, Dear Scarlett

CHAPTER ONE

On Parents

Dear Chandler, Dear Scarlett:

Whatever you thought when you saw your parents for the first time, I promise you it was nothing compared to the excitement your parents felt when they saw you for the first time. You kept them waiting for nine months while they tried to figure out how big you would be, how cute you would be, and, of course, when they'd get to hold you and smother you with love.

Parents are a pretty important part of who you are because, without them, you wouldn't be here in the first place. (How that all happens we'll deal with later—your parents are hoping *much* later.) A parent's job doesn't end after you're conceived and born, though. You will find your mother and father very helpful in your early days, especially before you can walk, talk, feed, or clean yourself after you've engaged in the most elementary bodily functions.

And even if you didn't need your parents to provide your food, shelter, clothing, and medical care, you'd still want them around because they are incredibly entertaining. You must find it pretty funny when they talk to you in a baby voice, trying to explain things you can't possibly understand. "Does baby want to go to sleepy land?" I always thought it would be hilarious if God in His infinite sense of humor gave infants the ability to sit up in their cribs and declare, "No, I don't want to sleep—I just got here and I'm ready to PAR-TAY!" Talking to babies is kind of like talking to dogs. "Does Fluffy want to go for a walk?" Just once I want to hear a puppy say, "Not right now. I want to finish watching *Old Yeller* on cable."

The reason your parents talk to you like this is because they are actually losing the ability to have a rational adult conversation. They just don't know it. As funny as this is, you need to have some sympathy for them because ever since you came into the world, they've spent most of their time feeding you, clothing you, cleaning you, changing your diaper, putting you to bed, and protecting you from cold viruses and grandparents. And even when they're not doing these things, they're thinking about doing them, or dreaming about doing them, or talking about doing them. So, basically, you've taken over their brains.

And let me tell you, this distraction can often lead parents to do some pretty dumb things.

Before your uncle John Mark was born, I knew I would be totally new to the parenting thing and didn't have the first clue what I'd be doing. I spent months reading every book I could get my hands on about how to take care of a baby. By the time the baby came, I thought I was basically ready for anything—from his stepping on a rusty nail to breaking his arm to throwing a tantrum in public. What I wasn't prepared for was being thrust into a life-or-death situation that would forever change my understanding of fatherhood.

One day I was standing over John Mark's crib when he was just a few days old, changing his diaper, when suddenly his chest collapsed. It happened so quickly, and even though his chest quickly returned to its original position, I was worried. What had just happened did not look natural. Then, before I could scream for his mother, an ambulance, or perhaps the national guard, it happened again. When I saw my baby son's tiny little chest cave in a second time, I mustered all the volume I had in my voice and yelled to your grandmother, "JANET! COME HERE NOW! CALL 911! JOHN MARK IS HAVING A HEART SEIZURE!" I continued my panicked cry for help until your grandmother arrived. Just then, John Mark's chest collapsed again. "That is a hiccup," your grandmother calmly informed me before walking out of the room and leaving me to my diaper-changing duties.

"Hiccup? Are you sure?" I called out at her. I thought she was being rather cavalier about our first and only child's possible collapsed lung or cardiac arrest. I had hiccupped plenty of times in my life, and my chest never touched my spine because of it!

But she was right—it was just a hiccup. I had been so worried about having to save my child from a life-threatening injury that I had lost all common sense. So when your parents overreact to some things, as they will, forgive them. No one is great at something on the first try, and parenting requires a person to deal with a whole lot of surprises—some good, some bad. You may laugh at them sometimes (as will I, because I know what it's like), but I promise, if you ever have children, you'll understand.

Beyond providing you with basic economic and physical necessities, as well as twenty-four-hour live interactive entertainment, parents will give you something you need more than anything else: unconditional love.

You probably already know your parents love you. They tell you all the time and they treat you as if you were the center of the universe (which, to them, you are). But it's the unconditional aspect of this love that you probably won't fully grasp until much later on. I hope your parents are still around when that happens so you can tell them you finally understand and let them know how much you love them, too.

Unconditional love means that your parents don't love you because you're cute (even though you are), or because you're intelligent (of course you are!), or because you have amazing talents to sing or play sports (I'm sure you do!). They don't love you because you make their lives easier. In fact, when you first showed up, you were pretty much useless. You couldn't help out around the house, and yet you still demanded constant attention and care. If that wasn't enough, you kept your parents up all hours of the night, and because they had to take care of you all the time, they didn't have time to do a lot of the things they used to do, like go out to eat or have leisurely conversations with their adult friends. You pretty much upended whatever serenity they had.

You certainly aren't loved because of your financial contribution to the family. Your parents would probably never smile at you if they fully understood the costs associated with bringing you into this world. Your parents could shop at fine jewelry stores on a weekly basis and have lobster flown in each Friday from Maine with the money it will cost to properly provide for your every need and desire. With food, clothing, medical bills, day care, and education, not to mention all the hobbies and toys you'll want throughout your childhood, your cost to your parents will be staggering. But even if they got a bill for your next twenty-two years of life support and the cost of your education, they still wouldn't put you on eBay.

No, this love you receive by the truckload is not your parents' way of thanking you because you've proved yourselves economically, politically, or socially useful. Your parents love you simply because you're their children, and that will never change. Nothing you do will make them love you more, and nothing you do will make them love you less. Now, you can do some things that might make them *like* being around you more or less, but their love is pretty well set. Even if you break their hearts (and you'd better not!), they will still love you, forever and always.

I'm often amazed my own parents never left me on the doorstep of an adoption agency with a note encouraging some nice family to take me home and try to train me in the art of being a civilized human being. I was so rambunctious, my mother would sometimes ask, "Were you raised by wolves?" "No, not wolves," I told her. "Just you and Dad." That *really* made her mad, but I thought it was a perfectly legitimate response to what seemed like a really ridiculous question.

It's a good thing eBay wasn't around when I was little, because my parents would probably have tried to auction me off for a minimum bid of three dollars. And on some days, that would have been asking too much. Like the day Rosalind Doyle and I got in trouble for throwing rocks at cars driving past our house. Rosalind was my next-door neighbor's granddaughter, and she spent a lot of time at her grandparents' house. She was one day older than me, so we had a connection right off the bat. She was a beautiful young girl, but at age four I didn't care so much about that. All I cared about was that she really knew how to throw a rock. So there we stood in her grandparents' gravel driveway, throwing handfuls of loose gravel at passing cars as hard as our little arms would let us. We thought the sound of rock on metal was pretty cool. And we thought we were pretty cool, too—right up until we pelted the car of the local municipal judge, the Honorable John Wilson. As if that weren't bad enough, Judge Wilson knew my parents, and told them what Rosalind and I had done. Darn the luck! How were we supposed to defend ourselves against a judge? I wasn't going to be able to talk my way out of that one. And I didn't.

In those days, corporal punishment was the preferred method of responding to bad behavior. Today, it's almost unheard of, but when I was growing up, most parents assumed it was the best—sometimes the only—way to send a message and correct deviant behavior. That day I thought my parents were going to extend corporal punishment to make it capital punishment! Fortunately, an old-fashioned spanking (and a good one!) was the limit of the punishment.

While I was growing up, I got more than my share of spankings, and even though I didn't enjoy it, I survived just fine. I eventually came to realize that my parents didn't discipline me because they hated me and enjoyed seeing me in pain. It was exactly the opposite. They disciplined me because they loved me.

I don't expect you'll understand or express gratitude when your parents discipline you. It's never fun to get punished, but that's the point. Your parents discipline you so you learn the consequences of bad behavior now, when your offenses are relatively minor, instead of later, when your bad behavior could lead you to jail, or worse. So whenever your parents tell you, "One day you'll thank me for this!" you might not thank them right away, but, trust me, one day you will.

While we're discussing your parents, you might as well know something about your ancestry. I wasn't sure if I should bring this up, but one day you might run for political office, so it's probably best you hear everything from me rather than read it in the papers. I'll start by saying the same thing my dad (your great-grandfather Dorsey Huckabee) once said to me: "Son, don't look too far up your family tree—there's stuff up there you don't want to see!" He then explained that some of our ancestors were horse thieves, which in the days of the frontier was considered a heinous crime because people needed horses to travel and work the land. I'm not sure I believe this story, however, because my entire childhood I begged to have a pony. I figured that if my ancestors were so good at stealing horses, my dad could have at least picked up a pony somewhere. But the best I got was one of those broomstick-like things with a stuffed toy horse head on top. I never did get a real pony.

Your ancestors on my side of the family weren't exactly the most impressive folks. They didn't come over on the *Mayflower* or carry the blue blood of European nobility. They were never commissioned by a king or queen of some country to establish a colony of well-dressed, properly educated, and erudite ladies and gentlemen. No, my family was more blue collar than it was blue blood. From what we know, the Huckabees arrived on the shores of Georgia in the late 1700s and early 1800s to either avoid or escape the debtor prisons of England. Apparently, they had tried to go to Ireland first, but were turned away. So they booked passage on ships that pretty much dumped them off in a swamp where they learned that fighting mosquitoes was as difficult as fighting the British authorities. But poverty and hardship made them resilient, and a lot of those traits are probably still flowing through you. You'll need them for the world you face, so I hope you've inherited the grit and gravel that helped your forebears survive the tough and tumultuous American frontier. They may not have been well educated, prestigious, or wealthy, but they knew how to survive, and that's all that mattered.

Your grandpa (that would be me) was the first male in our family to graduate from college, but I was also the first to finish high school. My dad would have liked to have gotten a diploma, but in his day an education wasn't as critical for making a living, and usually only the privileged could afford to go to college. When World War II broke out, he went to work in the shipyards in Houston and never finished school. You shouldn't be ashamed of that, though. It took a long time for our family to reach the milestone of a college degree, but now that this path has been established, it will be up to you to make sure you do even better. Your ancestors suffered from poverty and lack of opportunity, but they still managed not only to survive, but also to pave the way for every generation after them to have the things they lacked. If not for them, you wouldn't be here, or, at least, you wouldn't be in such a good situation. You were born into a family who loves you and can take care of you, and you live at a time when you have more opportunity than anyone who has lived before you. Imagine all the things you can do. Your parents and your grandparents are all blessed to have received a college education. You should never take it for granted.

Never be embarrassed by your family history. Like your great-grandfather, I love to joke about the horse thieves, drunkards, gamblers, and all-around rowdies who certainly came before us. But for the most part, the Huckabees were hardworking people who mostly kept to themselves and yet always treated others with fairness and respect. They may not have been rich in pocket, but they were rich in spirit, never giving up on themselves or their communities. Hopefully, some of that same rugged spirit is deep within you. Should you ever run for public office, play sports, or start a business, you'll need it to go forward in the face of hardship and opposition. Without it, you're likely to be walked over while everyone else gets to where they want to go. Somehow, I think you'll both be fine.

But always remember that you had nothing to do with who your ancestors were or what they did. You do, however, have *everything* to do with what *you* decide to do with your life. Cherish the parts of your heritage that are worth holding on to. As for the parts you'd rather forget, the best way to separate yourself from them is to live such a big and wonderful life that people will only remember you for you.

Out of all the things your ancestors gave you, the best was your parents, who in turn gave you the chance to live what will hopefully be a long and joyous life. You are both blessed with really great parents. I know that because half of them were trained for their jobs by me.

Your parents are far from perfect, but one thing I know for sure—they love you unconditionally and totally. They will never abandon you, and while you might disappoint them from time to time, they will always love you no matter what. You will probably get angry at them sometimes, and you'll probably even think they are unfair when they say no, but they used to think I was unfair, too. Now they probably think I was right after all. You might think that yourself someday!

CHAPTER TWO

On Education

Dear Chandler, Dear Scarlett:

Scarlett, one afternoon when your mother was six years old and had just completed the first grade, she and I were sitting on the patio when she matter-of-factly told me, "I'm not going back to school next year. I've had enough." I kept myself from laughing, but made it clear to her that she would most certainly be going back to school the next year, and the next, and the next, until she graduated. In fact, Sarah not only completed the second grade, but was an excellent student through high school, had a great experience in college, and even graduated from Ouachita Baptist University as the student body president.

Chandler, your dad, David, wasn't nearly as interested in school as I'd hoped he would be. But he ultimately went to college and served as student goverment president. Truth is, he chose Arkansas State University largely due to its proximity to prime duck-hunting land and scheduled his classes so as to maximize his early morning hunting. To this day, stories still float around the campus about the governor's son coming to class with muddy hunting boots. But at least with constant prodding from your grandmother and me, he did eventually graduate. He turned out just fine!

I hope your parents have realized the importance of education since their earlier days, but just in case, I want to make a few things clear. There are a lot of ignorant people in the world, but the most dangerous people you'll ever encounter are the ones who don't know what they don't know. These people think they know everything and so refuse to seek counsel or ask questions. They are very confident, but that confidence often leads them to do dumb things.

Chandler, when your dad was young, he was in the Boy Scouts and worked each summer as a counselor at the Boy Scout camp. It was a wonderful experience that taught him a lot about nature and life, and, in his mind, pretty much everything about everything.

One day, our family and several friends of ours were staying at a house we owned on Lake Greeson in southwest Arkansas and decided to clear off and burn some brush and old limbs from the property. Your dad, who was seventeen at the time, decided that stoking the fire the old-fashioned way, by letting it burn slowly and occasionally prodding the wood to spread the flame, was just too inefficient. So he decided to pour some white gas into the fire. White gas is an incredibly flammable fuel, and your grandmother Janet warned him to be careful and not pour the gas directly on the fire. Of course, your dad took umbrage at the idea that his mother would tell him how to do something he had been doing for years in the Boy Scouts. So in a tone we had become all too familiar with, your dad exclaimed, "Mother, I am a professional fire builder," as he simultaneously poured the white gas into the flame.

The instant those words exploded from his mouth, there was another explosion—a ball of orange flame fifteen feet high and twenty feet across that burst upward with a BOOM! For a second, we lost sight of your dad, and then he came forward from the ball of fire with the most surprised, and unusually humble, expression on his now eyebrowless face. After we made sure he and everyone else was okay, we all had yet another explosion—this one of ground-shaking laughter. For the rest of my life, I will never forget the look on your dad's face once he realized there was at least one thing he didn't know too well after all.

This story is funny only because no one was hurt. But people who don't know what they don't know can do a lot of harm. A doctor who doesn't know what he doesn't know could kill you. A pilot who doesn't know what he doesn't know could crash the plane. Even an accountant who doesn't know what he doesn't know can cost you your life savings, forcing you to eat cold beans from a can and Dumpster dive just to find stuff to wear.

That's why education is important. An educated person is certainly not someone who knows everything—no such person exists. An educated person is someone who knows how much she doesn't know and spends her entire life learning it.

I've already told you that you don't come from a long line of scholars, and that I was the first man in my family to finish high school and go to college. Sure, I could have decided to bypass an education and go to work in the fields after the seventh grade like my ancestors did, but the difference between them and me is that my parents and grandparents and great-grandparents didn't have any other choice. You do.

Actually, you don't. Because even if one day you decide, like Scarlett's mom, that you've had enough school, we're not going to let you stop going. The Huckabees worked hard for almost two hundred years to break the cycle of poverty and lack of education, and we're not about to let you put us on a backward slide without a fight!

You might not believe this, especially when you're sitting through a boring lecture or have been assigned piles of homework, but in most places of the world, kids like you would give anything to go to school. As an American you are lucky because no matter how much money you have or how naturally smart you are, you are able to get twelve years of education absolutely free. You don't have to shell out coins or bills from your pocket every time you go to school like you do when you go to a movie or a concert. In some countries, you have to prove you are in the top percentage of your peer group in order to be admitted to school. So I hope that instead of complaining about school, you'll get on your little knees every night and thank God and the United

States of America that you are fortunate enough to have an education available.

Of course, going to school won't make you smart unless you make the most of it. That's a lesson I learned the summer of 1973, right before I started my first year of college. My family was friendly with a local attorney named Talbot Field. Mr. Field had known my family for years and was aware that, as proud as my parents were that I was going to college, they couldn't give me any advice about what to expect because neither of them had ever been. So one day he called and asked if I would go get a Coke with him. ("Get a Coke" is Southern-speak for "have a conversation." In some parts of the country people "meet for coffee" or have a "conference." In the South, we "get a Coke.")

Talbot Field had been the state representative to the Arkansas legislature from our area and was a highly respected lawyer and community leader. I was flattered he would take any time with me at all. We rode around in his car for a while before ending up at the local Dairy Queen. After engaging in some small talk and asking me what I hoped to do with my life, Mr. Field said, "Mike, college will not teach you all you need to know. That's not the purpose of a good education. An education isn't about learning everything you'll ever need to know. It's about learning how to learn. You will spend the rest of your life learning. You are not going to college just to be a student for a few more years; you're going so you can prepare for the rest of your life. You never stop learning."

Simple stuff. Powerful stuff. Sure, one day you will receive a diploma and a handshake for completing a phase of your education, but that's just a formality. Your education doesn't ever end. In fact, the ceremony for a graduation is called "commencement," which doesn't mean "conclusion," but "beginning." Your education doesn't finish at graduation; it begins.

A good education isn't one that forces you to memorize facts and figures, but one that teaches you how to learn. Learning is hard work. It's not enough to sit in a classroom or read a book. You have to study, think deeply, and ask questions. If you can train yourself to do this, you will be able to apply those skills to all aspects of your life. Learning is about noticing things, paying attention not only to the big pieces, but to the little ones. When you do that, you learn. And the more you train yourself to observe and notice, the better you will understand the world around you.

I had to write a lot of term papers in college, but it took me years before I finally realized that the real purpose of doing a research paper wasn't to learn something about a topic, but to learn how to research. As a member of the debate team, I learned that all the preparation involved in preparing my arguments was not about advocating for a particular viewpoint; it was about learning *how* to advocate for a viewpoint by using and organizing facts.

Mind you, the type of research I did in school was much more labor intensive than what you have to do today. If I wanted to look something up, I had to go to the library and browse through articles and books in the card catalog—by hand! When composing a paper, I had to write in longhand on a yellow legal pad and then type it on a portable Smith-Corona electric typewriter. Boy, what I could have done with Google and a MacBook Pro back in 1973!

Years later, as a governor, I had to analyze vast amounts of material to make tough decisions. Some of these were literally life-or-death decisions—for example, when I had to review the case files for convicted criminals and determine whether they should receive the death penalty or another sentence. There wasn't a day in my job that my ability to think critically and objectively wasn't vital.

You will be a learner for life, and if you are really smart, you will try to learn something new every day. Life is short and there is no way to learn everything, so shouldn't you make the most of it? Learning is like being told you have one hour to go through the mall and buy as much as you want. What would you do? Would you wander aimlessly through the halls, stopping at Auntie Anne's for a pretzel? Or would you rush to your favorite stores, scooping up all the toys and trinkets you love?

The difference here is that there is much more knowledge in the world than there is stuff at the mall. And the stuff you put in your brain is going to get you a lot further in life than any material thing. The more knowledge you have, the more you are able to do. You can get better jobs and understand more things.

The stuff you learn in school is not the only education worth having. There are so many different types of knowledge, each of them valuable in its own way. As you go through life, you'll meet people with less formal education than you, but that doesn't mean they are stupid. Some of the smartest people I've ever known didn't have a degree from anywhere but the University of Life, where they learned things no book or professor could ever have taught them.

There is a wonderful lady in De Valls Bluff, Arkansas, named Miss Mary, who has a little building behind her house. It's a humble shack with not much to it except a rather crudely hand-painted sign hanging from the side of the building that reads simply, "Pie Shop." Miss Mary has been making pies for nearly fifty years, and out of her pie shop come the best homemade pies I've ever had.

I remember the first time I had her coconut pie. The meringue was so light and airy it seemed three feet tall and the pie tasted as perfect as any pie could. But Miss Mary also makes a southern specialty that is becoming a lost art: fried fruit pies. For the uninitiated, a fried pie is not a dessert, but a work of art. When done right, the outer shell is flaky and tastes lightly of flour, while the apple, peach, or other fruit filling is hot and gooey inside. I know this is how fried fruit pies are supposed to taste because that's how Miss Mary makes them.

Now, I wouldn't ask Miss Mary to teach me the "hermeneutics of rabbinical exegesis" as practiced in the time of King David. Nor would I trust her to explain molecular biology or nuclear fission to me (if you ask me what molecular biology and nuclear fission are, I'll tell you to go ask your science teachers). But if I wanted to learn how to make the most delicious, beautiful, and near perfect pies on this planet, I'd sit down with Miss Mary around her cookstove in the little building behind her house on Highway 70 and ask her to show me how it's done. She would probably explain the art of a perfect meringue, or the best temperature at which to cook an apple pie, or even the secret to a chocolate filling that isn't sticky. None of this knowledge saves lives, but what Miss Mary does in her little pie kitchen requires as much skill as a surgeon and as much art as a virtuoso pianist. Yes, her pies are *that* good!

Maybe the surgeon's work will do more good (especially for one's arteries), but I wouldn't ask *him* to make me a pie. (For the record, I wouldn't ask Miss Mary to take out my gall bladder, either!) The point is some people do work that requires more formal schooling or that pays more money or that gets them more accolades from the public. But the beautiful thing about knowledge is that there's enough for everyone, and we all have something to teach one another.

Another thing I want you to understand is the distinction between intelligence and education. Some people are really well educated but aren't that smart when it comes to doing much with what they know. An education is valuable only if you use it to do something worthwhile. I've known people with advanced doctoral degrees who couldn't hold a decent job because of their total lack of people skills or their lack of common sense. And some of the most successful people I've met barely had an eighth-grade education. What they lacked in formal education, they made up for with experience, hard work, and an innate entrepreneurial brilliance.

I'm not saying these people were better off without school. On the contrary, they succeeded *in spite of* their lack of education, not because of it. And the people I know all wish they had enjoyed a greater level of education. Some of them have even invested millions of dollars of their own money in schools and colleges so that young people in their communities will have the advantages they lacked.

J. B. Hunt, founder of the famed trucking company by the same name; Harvey and Bernice Jones, who created the Jones Trucks Line; and John Tyson, who launched Tyson Foods and turned it into the world's largest producer of meat, all lacked college degrees and yet have endowed colleges and universities with millions of dollars. Each of them valued education, but didn't have access to it—a common problem back in the day, when many families lived modest lives and even the children lucky enough to finish high school were expected to get a job right after graduation so they could help pay the bills. But Hunt, the Joneses, and Tyson were naturally intelligent, curious, hardworking, and willing to take great risks because they had nothing to lose. So before you get any wise ideas of quitting school to start a trucking company, remember that you're blessed. The closest you'll probably come to deprivation is having to settle for a single serving of ice cream when you come to visit Grandpa. And I'm guessing I'll be such a pushover that I'll probably give in anyway.

Another wonderful thing about school is the people in it. Yes, your teachers are (hopefully) great, but you can also learn a lot from your classmates. The other people you share the planet with act and think differently than you do. Learning to respect and understand them is one of the most valuable lessons of your life.

Some people are going to be better than you at certain things (although I can't imagine who or what that would be!), and you are going to be better than them at other things. There will probably be some kids you go to school with who never sweat. I knew kids like that when I was little. I never understood it. On the hottest day of the year, when we'd play hard on the playground and most of my classmates and I looked like we'd just been rescued from a six-month stint in the Sahara, some kids would look like they'd just stepped off the page of a catalog. Maybe you'll be one of those kids. But even if you are, I hope you won't avoid the smelly, sweaty kids, because I'm sure they'll be able to teach you something, too.

When I was in junior high school, I had a friend named Gary Barham with whom I played guitar. Gary and I were the same age, but he had started playing a couple of years before me and came from a musical family—his older brother and cousin were musicians who played in one of the local rock bands. Gary was a gifted musician, and when we first started playing music together, he was so much better than I was that I was a little intimidated. But instead of being embarrassed and running off to play guitar alone in my room where no one could hear, I used him as motivation. Gary's superior skills inspired me to practice until I could play as well as he could. Gary and I eventually started our own band when we were in the seventh grade, and we continued for almost three years until we both gravitated to other bands that needed us.

It's human nature to want to be the best at everything, and you should constantly strive to improve on the things that are important to you. But if everyone was great at everything, we would all be the same and the world would be very boring. Don't ever get discouraged if you're not good at something immediately, or if someone is better than you at something. If God wanted you to be someone else, He certainly could have made you that person. But He made you to be *you*. I hope your education will make you a better student for life, but I also hope it makes you smart enough to realize just how special you are.

I said earlier that learning is like being given a cart you can fill with whatever you want. What you put in your cart will reflect not only what you think is important and reveal your level of judgment, but it will also shape your future and largely determine where you end up down the line. Why waste time when you're young and have to go to school for at least thirteen years anyway? Better start filling up that cart!

CHAPTER THREE

On Work

Dear Chandler, Dear Scarlett:

You guys are a long way from having to worry too much about work—though I'm sure before too long your parents will start telling you to do a few things that will *feel* like a lot of work. First, you'll have to do things like pick up your toys once you're finished playing with them, feed the dog, brush your teeth, and put your dirty clothes in the laundry basket before you go to bed at night. As you get a little older, you'll probably have to help with yard work, clean up the dinner dishes, and wash the car. The funny thing is, you'll beg to do these things when you are too little, and then complain about how much you hate them when you are old enough.

As much as I'm going to enjoy watching your parents

deal with the same complaints they made to me when they were young, fair warning: Whining doesn't make the work disappear and it doesn't make it easier. You're going to have to do things you don't want to do, so I highly recommend another approach to work. Not only will this make you tolerate the little chores your parents make you do, but it might even make you learn to love doing them.

You probably don't believe me, but I promise I'm not crazy. A man named John Ruskin, who died more than 150 years before you were born, once said, "The highest reward for man's toil is not what he gets for it, but what he becomes by it."

When you're young, you do things you don't want to do because someone else—your parents, a teacher, or some other adult—tells you to. But even if your parents never made you lift a finger, even if you never had to clean your room or mow the lawn or wash the dinner plates, at some point in your life you're going to have to work. Your parents are not going to be able to take care of you forever, and while you may not realize it anytime soon, the little annoying chores you do now will prepare you for much harder—and more important—work later on.

One thing that won't change as you get older is that

people will still love to complain about work. But successful, happy people know that work is not just some terrible burden you suffer so you don't starve or wind up sleeping on a park bench. Nor is it something you do so you can make lots of money and buy more stuff. Work is a force that shapes your character and gives you self-esteem, which is essential to having a fulfilled and successful life. Self-esteem is basically confidence in yourself—the knowledge that you can take care of yourself and accomplish things without help from others. It's the feeling a farmer gets when he brings in his crop, or the feeling a musician gets when he receives a standing ovation at the end of a performance, or the feeling a soldier gets when awarded the Medal of Honor.

There really is something very satisfying about setting a goal, working hard to achieve it, and then being able to look at the finished product and say, "It is good." In fact, that's exactly what God did right after He finished creating the world. He decided He wanted to design something so He wouldn't have to be alone anymore. So He got to work making the universe, the planet Earth, all the animals and plants, and, most important, human beings like you and me. When He finished, He looked at everything He'd accomplished and said, "It is good."

I believe we are hardwired to find fulfillment in our labor, and having a job and doing something productive—whatever it is—gives a person a sense of purpose. In my experience, people who are good at what they do can find pleasure in their work. On Sixth Avenue and Forty-seventh Street in New York City, just across the street from the Fox News studios where I work, there is a delightful young man who sets up his shoe shine stand each day. I go regularly to get my shoes shined by him because not only does he do a great job, he does it with an outgoing and cheerful spirit. Yes, I'm sure he does this on purpose, knowing that a friendly attitude will result in repeat customers and bigger tips. But he still seems far happier than most of the people I see coming out of the offices of the prestigious financial firms in the buildings nearby. These people may be dressed in two-thousand-dollar suits and carrying five-hundred-dollar Italian leather briefcases, but they don't seem happy at all. They may have fancy, important jobs, but they don't love their work. It just goes to show that a job is only as good as the satisfaction you get from doing it.

The key thing to remember is that *you* have to do the work yourself in order to derive the benefits from it.

Some people will try to build your self-esteem for you. They may think that "everyone deserves a trophy" because if someone tells a child he isn't perfect at everything and that he should try to do better next time, he'll be scarred for life. I hope you don't fall for this nonsense. It won't kill you to lose at something or receive a low grade on a test you didn't study for. But it might kill you to think you can give a halfhearted effort and still receive the same reward for your efforts as those who've tried their hardest. Find something you are good at, work hard to be the best you can be, and enjoy the accolades. That will make you feel so much better about yourself than any fake trophy, and it will prepare you for the "real world," where people aren't as patient with those who don't pull their own weight.

Let me clarify something: Just because work is rewarding doesn't mean it's always fun. In fact, work was originally invented as a punishment. By now you've probably heard the story of Adam and Eve. When God created the earth He decided to make two beings who were alike in His image. So He got down in the dirt and made Adam, the first man, and out of Adam's rib He made Eve, the first woman. Sounds a little rough, but life was good for them for a while because God let them live in the Garden of Eden, a paradise where every need was taken care of.

God pretty much gave Adam and Eve a life of complete leisure. He fed them with abundant food that required no farming, shopping, cooking, or cost. And they didn't even need clothing! Just think of all the money your parents would have saved on your cute little baby outfits if you could have crawled around in your birthday suit. And that doesn't even begin to start adding up what your *grandparents* would have saved on those cute little baby outfits!

Adam and Eve had a cushy life, to say the least. They could do anything they wanted with one and only one exception. They were forbidden to eat the fruit of *one* very particular tree—the Tree of Knowledge of Good and Evil. This was just one tree in a pretty amazing garden with a virtually unlimited array of tasty fruits, vegetables, and nuts. Should have been an easy rule to follow, right? Wrong. One day a serpent came to them and told them that God was being unfair by not allowing them to eat from that tree. Once he made them doubt God and believe they might be missing something, the serpent said, "God doesn't want you to be as smart as

Him. That's why He doesn't want you to eat that fruit."

You'll probably read stories or hear people say that Adam and Eve "ate an apple" and that's what got them into trouble. Kids have been using that line for hundreds of years to try to get away with eating candy instead of apples, but there's nothing in the Bible at all about an apple. The reason God didn't want Adam and Eve to eat the fruit of the Tree of Knowledge of Good and Evil wasn't because He didn't want them to eat apples; He didn't want them to know the difference between right and wrong because he wanted them to trust Him to take care of that for them.

It's just like when your parents tell you not to put your hand on a hot stove. They don't tell you that because touching a hot stove is such a fun thing to do and, in their irrational meanness and dislike for you, they are afraid you'll like it when your burn your fingers on hot metal. No, they tell you this because they love you a lot and don't want to hear you cry and see the little blisters form on your perfect, tiny hand.

What God did to punish Adam and Eve for their disobedience was kind of like your parents saying, "Fine, you don't believe I know what's best for you? Then go ahead and see what happens when you touch the hot stove." Except He said, "So, you want to experience things for yourself? You don't think everything I've provided for you is good enough? Then I'll show you what it's like to have to keep this place up, tending the Garden instead of just eating everything in it."

From that day forward, we've been working.

We can shake our fists at Adam and Eve all we like, but people have done that for thousands of years and it hasn't changed a thing. We still have to work to feed, shelter, and clothe ourselves, so we might as well make the best of it. And the good news is, if you go about it right, your work can become one of the great pleasures of your life.

I can't remember a time in my life when I didn't do some kind of work. When I was very little, I did the work my parents made me do. I made my bed, raked leaves, put away dishes, and—my least favorite job of all, which thank goodness came only once a year— picked up pecans from the pecan trees in our yard.

Today, I'd love to have pecan trees in my yard. (Not that I would pick up the pecans; I'd make my grandchildren do that!) But each fall when I was little, my parents would give me and my sister, Pat, large paper sacks from the grocery store, and the two of us would trot out to the yard to pick up the pecans that had fallen from the tree so our mom could shell and roast them. We spent hours bending over and digging through the leaves to find every single pecan until not a single one was left. We didn't get paid for our trouble—we were told that if we wanted to eat that night and sleep in a bed instead of in the yard, we'd pick up the pecans. Even though I loved my mother's roasted pecans, the unpleasant memories of having to spend my Saturdays (my only day off from school and church, for heaven's sake!) picking up pecans made me avoid them until I became a grown-up and rediscovered how delicious they are.

I found out early in life that there are two kinds of work: the kind you do because you have to (like picking up pecans in the yard) and the kind you do because you want something bad enough to work really hard for it. Long before I ever worked a real, paying job, I found some ways to earn money to get the things I wanted.

In the "old days," when your grandpa was your age, people drank soft drinks from glass bottles instead of aluminum cans or plastic bottles. But instead of throwing the empty bottles away, people returned them to the store, where they were sent back to the soft drink bottling company to be used over and over. Imagine drinking a Coke—in the South, we called all soft drinks "Coke," even if it was a Pepsi, an Orange Crush, or an RC Cola—from a bottle that had probably been used fifty times by fifty other people before you! (Don't worry—it was thoroughly washed and cleaned each time.) Long before people started recycling because it's good for the environment, we recycled bottles because it was the only way to make sure there would be more Cokes! Okay, I'm sure the soft drink industry would probably have kept making bottles, but we weren't so sure back then.

The best part of recycling was that for each bottle returned to the store, you received two cents. (Today you get a nickel, but this was a long time ago.) I had a little red wagon that I would tie to my bicycle and pull behind me whenever I would go searching for bottles that people had thrown on the side of the street. Nowadays, people pick up bottles on the side of the road in order to keep neighborhoods clean and to protect the environment. Back then I did it because it was the only way I could earn money! I guess the litter collectors of today have a good motivation, too, but I'm not sure I would have ridden my bicycle all over town when I was seven years old just to be a good citizen.

Collecting Coke bottles was much harder work than picking up pecans. The bottles were usually dirty or sticky, and sometimes I had to dig them out from muddy ditches. I spent hours pulling my little red wagon up and down sidewalks or asking people if they had any old bottles they wanted to get rid of. Of course, most people had the same idea I did and would take their own bottles back for the deposit when they bought more soft drinks, especially if their families were as poor as we were. I learned to go to the nicer homes where the more well-off people lived to try to talk them out of their bottles. Some of them were glad to have some scruffy kid take the dirty bottles away. Not too many, but enough to make it worth ringing their doorbells.

It was hard work to collect bottles, but I bought my first catcher's mitt with the money I earned. I took great care of that catcher's mitt because I knew how hard I had worked to get the money to buy it. Coke bottles took me to the movies each Saturday (it was only twenty-five cents to get in, but still, that was thirteen bottles), got me into the public swimming pool in the summer, and even helped me buy my first real gun, a .22-caliber single-shot Springfield rifle that Chandler's dad now owns. Coke bottles helped me buy my first Beatles album, too, which was a big deal because the Beatles were my favorite band (and still are). I didn't realize it then, but collecting Coke bottles taught me a simple but very valuable lesson: that earning money was hard, but the harder and longer I worked, the more money I would make and the more I could do with it.

After a while, I tried more advanced schemes to earn money, such as selling things door-to-door, like greeting cards. At the age of eight, I became a bona fide sales representative of the Wallace Brown greeting cards company and would walk the neighborhood trying to persuade people to buy several boxes of greeting cards for birthdays, Christmas, or other occasions. Becoming a sales representative for Wallace Brown wasn't that hard. If you were willing to send in your name and address and promise to go banging on doors in the neighborhood, you, too, could become a "sales representative."

As I tried my best sales routine, most people would tell me no, and some slammed the door in my little eight-year-old face. I sold a few cards, but ultimately decided that either I wasn't the greatest door-to-door salesman, the cards weren't that good, or I was trying to sell cards to people who just couldn't afford or didn't need them.

I got my first "real" job, with a boss and a regular

paycheck, at the ripe old age of fourteen. The job was at the local radio station in Hope, Arkansas. KXAR was an AM radio station that operated during the day at 1490 on the radio dial. (Radios had dials then—not buttons.) It was a wonderful job that helped me learn how to speak eloquently, think on my feet, and react when things went haywire. I also learned what it was like to have others depend on me—my producers depended on me to fill the dead space, and our listeners depended on me to deliver news and information about our community. It was a lot of responsibility, but I learned a lot and have since loved being on air.

My radio career got started thanks to what, at the time, seemed like the worst thing that had ever happened to me. I was eleven years old and playing Little League baseball on a team sponsored by the Century Bible class of the local Methodist church. We were the worst in our league and hadn't won a single game the entire season. I was the catcher (though given how bad our pitching was, I was probably more of the "scooper," scooping up the ball from the dirt in front of home plate). On a summer night in June of 1967, a young man named Mark Cathey, playing for the team sponsored by Midwest Dairy, hit a foul tip that I tried to catch, foolishly, by using both hands. The ball came right off his bat and directly into the index finger on my right—mitt-free—hand. My finger pretty much shattered and was bent completely backward, pointing over the back of my hand. That ended my season and pretty much any hopes I had to one day take the St. Louis Cardinals to another World Series.

Because I couldn't play anymore, the coach suggested I help out in the press box at the Little League park by being one of the people who announced the batters over the loudspeakers. In return, I would be able to watch the games and get free Cokes from the concession stand. My hometown was so small that the local radio station broadcast the Little League games live on the radio. One night when I was announcing the batting order, the person who normally did the broadcasts for the station called in sick, so the station manager, Haskell Jones, came to the park to call the play-by-play of the game. Perhaps because Haskell couldn't think of many things worse than having to describe eleven- and twelve-year-old boys playing baseball, or perhaps because he was just trying to be funny, he turned to me and said, "Hey, kid, how would you like to call a few innings of play-by-play on the radio?"

"Sure!" I said. I called a few innings, and after a while Haskell said, "Kid, you're not bad. If you'd like to work in radio, come see me when you turn fourteen and can get your FCC license."

I took him at his word, and in the few months before I turned fourteen, I often went to the radio station to sit with the disc jockeys and news people and learn how to "run the board"—radio slang for operating the massive console that controlled the tape machines, the record turntables (yes, it was so long ago that music was actually played from vinyl discs called records), and the various sources that fed network news, phone lines, and commercials. Within days of my birthday, I took the FCC exam to become a fully licensed operator of a radio station.

Working at the local radio station in those days was a pretty heady job for a kid. I did play-by-play sports in football, basketball, and baseball, was a nighttime and weekend disc jockey, read the news from the AP wire and the local news that we gathered at the station, read weather reports, and even voiced commercials. Most of the people in the community listened to KXAR during at least part of their day because it was the best and most immediate source of local news, weather, sports, and other information. In those days, people often learned about the deaths of their neighbors, because obituaries were read on the air, as were hospital admissions and discharges. It's hard to imagine being able to do this now, with all the privacy laws we have, but that's the way things were back then, and as a result I had the most high-profile job a junior high student could possibly have. And if that wasn't enough, the studio I worked in was air-conditioned!

My radio station job seemed especially glamorous when compared to my other job at the time—working at the local J.C. Penney store. If I was ever in danger of deluding myself that working at the radio station made me some sort of celebrity, my job at Penney's humbled me immediately.

I was the janitor who swept floors and cleaned windows and the glass doors. (To this day, I'm irritated when I see people put their grimy fingers on a store's glass door instead of the handles because I know some poor kid with a bottle of Windex will have to wipe off the fingerprints!) I also unloaded the trucks that delivered the new merchandise, made price tags, and stocked the store with the items. I wasn't allowed to wait on the customers—I was just the errand boy for the employees who did. Needless to say, I much preferred my job at the radio station, but that doesn't mean I hated working at Penney's. It was a fine company to work for and not just because I got a 15 percent discount on the stuff I bought there. I worked with a lot of wonderful people, but the thing that made the job so exceptional was that I got to work at a truly great company, which, thanks to its founder, James Cash Penney, had a special dedication to giving people good value for their money and providing middle-class and working people with good clothing at affordable prices.

Neither of these jobs paid very well. The station paid me minimum wage, which at the time was $1.30 per hour, but employers were allowed to pay 15 percent *below* that for students, so I earned only $1.10. Even with the two jobs combined, I couldn't afford fancy clothes or a slick sports car (at that age, I was still riding a bicycle anyway), but I was earning money—money that I used to start saving for college and pay for the things I wanted to do.

After working at KXAR and J.C. Penney, I headed to Ouachita Baptist University in Arkadelphia, Arkansas. I landed a job at the local radio station, KVRC, where I worked forty hours a week in addition to going to class full time. It was a rugged schedule. I usually had classes all day, starting at eight a.m., after which I would head to the station, stay on air until about eleven p.m., then head back to the dorm to study for a bit and get a little sleep before starting the routine all over.

I've worked hard since those teenage days, but I never resented having to work my way through college when other people were enjoying living off their parents' savings. The work ethic I learned out of necessity helped me get my four-year college degree in two and a half years and taught me that there is always a place in any organization for someone willing to work hard and go above and beyond what's expected of them.

I'm not telling you all this personal history just so you understand where your work DNA comes from. I'm telling you so you'll understand why I won't give you everything you want—even when I might be able to. My first job in radio paid little and demanded a lot of my time, but it gave me the skills I needed for the jobs in TV and radio I have today. These jobs have made it possible for me to give you everything you will need throughout your childhood and teenage years. But that would be the worst thing I could do for you.

Working hard teaches you independence, and what it

means to live a life worth living. You will be able to call the shots of your own life, you will be able to do whatever you love, and you will be able to decide how much time and effort you put into getting to where you want to go. If you relied on me—or anyone else—you'd always have to worry that something would happen. What if my producers decided they were sick of hearing me talk all the time? I'd be out of a job, and you would be on your own. Your grandpa wants to give you the world, and it's awfully tempting to give you things that I had to work so hard to get as a kid. But now that I'm older, I realize that the best things I got from my hard work were not a paycheck or a catcher's mitt, but a willingness to do whatever it took to accomplish my goals.

Having said all I've said, I think you'll understand what I mean, but here are a few more important principles I hope you'll keep in mind:

1. *No one owes you a job.*

A job is not a right, but a privilege. And if you accept a job from someone, you owe *them* for giving you the opportunity—not the other way around.

2. *Go to work early and stay late.*

You're probably not going to be fired because you came in too early, worked too hard, and stayed later than all the other employees. Five minutes early ought to be considered ten minutes late.

3. *Do your work.*

This should go without saying, but you'd be surprised how many people don't follow this rule. Don't do *your* thing on your employer's time. And instead of complaining about the small, annoying tasks that will probably be assigned to you when you first start out, do them so well that your employer decides you are too valuable to be wasted on such small things in the future. You will not be promoted by failing at the job you have. You get promoted for doing the job you have so well that people know you're capable of bigger and better things.

4. *Do the things you like least first.*

We all would prefer to do the things we like over the things we don't like, but if you do all the fun stuff first, the hard or boring stuff will just seem harder and more boring later. Get your least favorite tasks out of the way, and you'll have more time to do the things you actually like.

5. *No job is perfect.*

If you can find a job that will pay you more and let you work less, and which you enjoy, take it. But until that job comes along, be grateful for the one you have, regardless of what it is. If you don't like the job you have, you probably won't like the one you get next, either. If you really want to appreciate the boss you have, quit working for him and go work for yourself. Then you will appreciate the boss you had before.

6. *Don't brag.*

Don't try to get noticed or call attention to the job you are doing. If you are doing it well, people will notice. And you're more likely to be rewarded for doing a good job than for being obnoxious.

I'm not sure where you'll start out in your first job or what kind of job it will be, but I do know that if you exemplify the best work habits, you will end up at the top of your field. Grandpa will not get you there, but I will be extremely proud when you do.

CHAPTER FOUR

On God

Dear Chandler, Dear Scarlett:

There's a story I once heard about a little girl who was sitting in her first-grade class drawing a picture. When the teacher asked her, "What are you drawing?" the little girl replied matter-of-factly, "I'm drawing a picture of God." "Oh, honey," the teacher said. "No one knows what God looks like." Undeterred, the little girl continued to draw and bluntly responded, "Well, they will in a few minutes!"

You have to admire this little girl's confidence, even though it's probably a bit misplaced. No one can know what God looks like because He was smart enough to not tell us. He could have revealed Himself to us, but He worried that if He did, we'd just worship His image or make T-shirts with His face on them instead of properly honoring Him.

But just because we can't see Him or take a picture of Him doesn't mean we can't know God. In my previous letter, I told you how important knowledge is, but of all the things you will ever know, nothing is more important than knowing who He is, why He made you, and what your purpose is in His Creation. If you know these three things, you'll be a successful and contented person, no matter what else happens or fails to happen in your life. Knowing these three things will give you satisfaction whether you're rich or poor, famous or forgotten, loved or despised. Because a connection with God will help you truly understand and appreciate life.

Look around you. Everything that has ever been created was made for a specific purpose. A fork is created as a utensil to help us eat food. A piano is created to make beautiful music. A ballpoint pen is created so we can write down our thoughts and ideas and communicate with one another. Whether or not each of these things is effective depends on whether we use it for its intended purpose. If you try to use a fork to write a note, or use the piano to eat your food, or use a pen to make music, you won't get very far—and you'll probably look pretty silly in the process.

So think about it: If the inanimate things we see and use every day have a purpose, doesn't it stand to reason that the highest life form on earth—human beings— would have a purpose, too? If inventors make things to help them do something, wouldn't God—the most important inventor of all time—have created the universe and everything in it for the same reason?

I realize there are many who believe humans are just animated blobs that have evolved into something slightly more intelligent than the gooey mass of swamp scum we supposedly started as. These people think the idea of a God you can't see is so ridiculous that only blind faith could lead you to believe it was true. But in my opinion believing that something as significant as we are could evolve from a puddle of mud requires a far bigger leap of raw faith than accepting the logical conclusion that human beings did not spring into existence by accident, but were designed for a purpose. Even an ordinary object like a wristwatch or a table or a video game wasn't formed when random pieces of metal, plastic, wood, or thread crashed into one another in some uncontrolled explosion or collision. Each of these things was created when someone decided they would serve a great purpose and then carefully and cleverly designed and perfected each one. How il-logical and absurd is it to think there is purpose in a table, but no purpose for your life?

As I write this letter to you, I'm sitting on the beach by my house in Florida, gazing out at the ocean and the skies above it and marveling at the vastness of what is before me. There are thousands of living things in those waters and in the skies above. Each of them is part of an intricate, resilient, and yet delicate ecosystem in which all the various parts supply and support one another. Birds fly just above the surface of the water and then swiftly dive to catch fish that they will eat to stay alive. In turn, vegetation in the waters and other sea life feed the fish that feed the birds. Eventually, some of the fish will end up on my grill and on your plate and will provide delicious, nutritious protein to make your body healthy and strong. As you think about this delicate balance of life, ask yourself: Can something so perfect be created by accident?

And speaking of your body, what an amazing machine it is! Your eyes are more sophisticated than any camera ever manufactured. Your ears can hear an amazing range of sounds and recognize what they are. Your heart is an amazing system of circulatory pumps capable of taking the life-sustaining power of your blood and pushing it from the largest arteries in your chest to the tiniest capillaries in your eyes. Your lungs not only take in the oxygen you need to survive but filter it, expel the carbon dioxide, and clean the air around you as they complete this process.

Your brain is far more intricate than most computers could ever be, balancing thousands of conscious tasks like speaking and walking simultaneously, but also controlling the complex systems that allow you to feel pain and temperature, process light, breathe, and digest food. It also allows you to learn, remember, think, imagine, and do all the other things that separate us from every other being on the planet.

I hope you use your brain to its full capacity, not just while you're in school but throughout life. I especially hope you use the power of your own brain to conclude that God exists and that belief in Him is not just a result of faith and spirituality; it's a result of thoughtful reasoning made possible by the amazing intelligence only a supremely intelligent creator could bestow on you!

I'm not going to tell you what you should or should not believe. God does not want you to follow Him because you're forced to, but because you truly believe He exists and that you should obey His laws. You will puzzle over the mysteries of God your entire life, but for now, as you start your quest to know Him, I want you to consider a few things.

There either is a God or not—it's as simple as that. The hard part is choosing what to believe, and a lot changes when you accept the existence of God. Living a life of faith is not always easy or fun, because you are always accountable to someone. Sure, right now you're accountable to your parents and teachers, and when you grow up you'll certainly have more freedom to make your own choices than you do now. But even when you no longer have to live by your parents' rules, you'll always have to listen to God's.

If you don't believe in God, life becomes much easier, because you don't have to answer to a Supreme Being. Without a God to hold you responsible, any good deed or selfless action is unnecessary. Why would you give to the poor, hungry, or sick? Why would you join the military and risk your life to fight battles so that strangers can live in freedom? What would stop you from stealing from or harming someone else if the worst thing that would happen to you is that you would be arrested or have to pay a fine? Sure, no one wants to go to jail, but at least you won't be in jail for all eternity. And even if you suffer the ultimate consequence and lose your life, you don't need to worry about where your soul ends up because, if there is no God, that means you have no soul and your body will simply decay in the ground after you die.

Choosing to believe in God is just the first step toward knowing Him. If there is a God, He is either knowable or not. If He is not knowable—in other words, if He is a distant, impersonal, and uninvolved force that cannot or will not have a relationship with you—all you can do is hope that any interaction with Him is pleasant. An impersonal God relates to you in the same way an animal does: minding His own business until you get too close. If He *is* knowable and wants to have a relationship with you, nothing else you do in life is as important as establishing and nurturing that relationship.

This is another matter of simple common sense. For if there is a God big enough to create the world and all that is in it, that means He can destroy everything in it as well. If God can destroy all things, shouldn't you want to make sure you're on good terms with Him? Seriously, is there any relationship that could be more important? Is getting the autograph of a celebrity that big a deal? Is having dinner with Warren Buffett or Bill Gates as significant as knowing the Creator of the universe? Is having a closet full of the hottest fashions or driving a two-hundred-thousand-dollar car as big a deal as establishing a personal relationship with the Creator of All Things?

If we can know Him, then we need to determine *how* to do so. How has He revealed Himself to us and what are the rules we need to follow? As I have stated, the "case for God" rests largely in our observation of the world and the way it works. One of the main arguments for the existence of God is the fact that each of us has a conscience—that nagging voice inside our head that tells us it's wrong to hurt or cheat people even though sometimes we want to and it might make our lives easier. No one has to tell you these things are wrong, and most people don't refrain from doing bad things just because there are laws against them. Theologians and scholars call this "natural law," which is just a fancy way of saying there is something innate in us that leads us to agree on a moral code of conduct.

But just because we naturally know the difference between right and wrong doesn't mean it's natural for us to *behave* in accordance with natural law. Human beings are born selfish and, trust me, this includes you. I don't mean to suggest that right after you were born you sprawled in your crib like a diva and demanded Perrier chilled to exactly thirty-eight degrees and a bag of M&M's with all the green ones removed. All I mean is that, as exceptional as you are in every way to me, you share one particular quality with all other members of the human race: the expectation that people should take care of *you* first. When you were first born and wanted a fresh diaper or food, you didn't quietly raise your hand and ask in a soft and respectful tone, "If it's not too much trouble, would I perhaps be able to get a new diaper in the next few minutes?" Oh, no—it was more like "WAAAAAAAAHHHHHH!!!!!!!!!!! I want this nasty thing off and I want it off NOW!!!" You didn't know the words, but we all got the message.

That is the way you came into this world—with the spirit of "me first," if not "me only," with which we are all born. If you think you're somehow different, I hope I'm around when you get a peek at the first real group photo that you're in. It might be for your kindergarten class or your first T-ball team, but when the photo arrives and you see it for the first time, I'll bet you a fully paid college scholarship and the keys to a BMW convertible that you look for yourself first and then judge the quality of the photo based on how *you* look!

The Bible calls this our "sin nature," but that doesn't mean we are all natural-born serial killers or that we all want to rob people of their last dime or blackmail them into doing what we want. It just means we've all inherited a spiritual flaw that makes us think we are really important. And until we are humbled by an encounter with God, we pretty much stay that way.

It doesn't seem fair—if God didn't want us to be selfish, why did He make us that way? Well, He didn't originally. When God first created the world, He expected humans to trust in and follow Him without question. But then Adam and Eve rebelled, and like other things you inherited (like your grandpa's wit and sense of humor!), you inherited this sin nature. And until you decide to do something about it, you will live in rebellion against God and His plan.

I don't expect you to tame your little ego while you still need diaper changes and depend on your parents to feed you. But one day you might decide that you'll be better off serving God and listening to Him rather than pretending the universe revolves around you instead of God. When you make this decision, you will need to do the most unnatural thing a human being can do: You need to humble yourself and acknowledge that you need God more than He needs you. I hope I'm there when you decide that. In fact, I hope I can help you get to that day.

To start, let me explain what it means to serve God, because serving God is much different from serving anyone else. When you serve someone else, whether it's a boss or your parents or a teacher, you help give them the things they need and you do everything they tell you to do. But God does not *need* anything from you. So how do you serve Him?

Serving God simply means that you do what He does. I doubt He would clobber a kid on the playground or steal a kid's lunch money. You shouldn't, either. He wouldn't call a child a degrading name or try to humiliate a classmate. You shouldn't, either. He wouldn't break something and then lie about it to get out of trouble. You shouldn't, either.

He *would*, however, help someone who has fallen get up. And you should, too. He *would* offer His lunch to someone who didn't have any. And you should, too. He *would* defend someone who was being pummeled by a bully. And you should, too. He *would* sit with the kid in the lunchroom who usually sits by himself. And you should, too.

Serving God will help you build a better relationship with Him, and eventually you will come to really know Him. There are two ways to know someone. The first, most basic way is just knowing they exist. So if you meet someone at the playground and a few days later someone asks you, "Do you know Johnny?" You might say, "Yes! I just met him." The second way to know someone is much more important, because it involves building a relationship with someone and learning things about each other. From this type of knowledge spring trust and respect, which is vital to knowing God.

Let me tell you a story. One day when I was governor, a teenage girl arrived at the state capitol and went into the governor's office on the second floor. There were several layers of security between the front doors of the capitol and my desk, but this young lady was able to bypass all of them without so much as a second glance from the police and security team. She didn't have an appointment, so I was pretty surprised when I found her standing right beside me and asking for money. I gave her the money and she left the same way she came in with still no trouble from security.

Why was this young girl able to walk right into my office unannounced? Why did I hand over my hard-earned money to her? The reason was simple: That young lady was your mother, Scarlett! Sarah had come to the capitol, but not to see the governor, where it sometimes took weeks to get an appointment. She came to see her daddy, and she didn't have to have an appointment or go through security. The difference was that she had a special relationship with me. I knew her and trusted her and let her in without question.

This is the kind of relationship you want to have with God. You want to be able to talk to Him at any time and about anything without asking for permission first. And when you eventually pass into the next life, you want Him to see you, recognize you, know you, and welcome you into His Kingdom with open arms.

When I was a little kid, I never thought I would see a president of the United States in person, not even at a distance. That seemed impossible for someone who lived in an unimportant family in the little town of Hope, Arkansas. But I went on to meet every president from Gerald R. Ford up to our current president, Barack Obama. And what's more, they *know who I am* and call me by name.

I've met some famous people in my life—some I've gone on to know well and others I haven't seen since. But no meeting has had a greater effect on my life than the first time I met God. It was August 24, 1965, my tenth birthday, and I was attending vacation Bible school at the Garrett Memorial Baptist Church in Hope. I confess I didn't go to Bible school that day for spiritual reasons. I went because my sister, Pat, told me that at vacation Bible school the kids got to eat all the cookies and drink all the Kool-Aid they wanted and play baseball between classes. Sounded like a pretty good way to spend a birthday to me. It turned out I couldn't eat more than two cookies or drink more than one cup of Kool-Aid, but it didn't matter, because that day changed my relationship with God forever.

I had gone to Sunday school most Sundays and knew the stories of the Bible, but it wasn't until that day that the stories became real and personal and that I felt that I actually knew Jesus and not just about Him.

My faith has matured and grown over the years, but that doesn't mean I don't have my own doubts from time to time. The difference is that now my doubts aren't about whether there is or is not a God; they are about whether or not I'm following His teachings the best way possible. I know I can never be perfect, but every day I learn something new about God that brings me closer to truly knowing Him. I hope both of you develop a relationship with God, too. If you do, you won't need to draw a picture. You'll know Him in the most important way. You'll know him in your heart.

CHAPTER FIVE

On Loving Thy Neighbor

Dear Chandler, Dear Scarlett:

The older you get, the more rules you are going to have to follow. You might think life should work the opposite way—that when you're young, you'd have to obey a lot of rules because you're still learning how to behave properly, but as you mature, you'd be free to live by your own good judgment. Unfortunately, the simple rules you learn as a child—always say please and thank you, clean up your toys after you're done playing with them—are the easy ones. You'll know what I mean when you start doing taxes and have to learn the rules in sixty-seven thousand pages of tax law!

It wasn't supposed to be like this, because there's really only one rule that's necessary for living in a free and fair society. Unfortunately, most people haven't been able to follow it, so we had to make more rules to keep them in line. If we could all learn to live by this Rule to End All Rules, though, we'd be covered from stem to stern, from head to toe, from soup to nuts, from alpha to omega.

We haven't been able to figure this out for millennia, so we're probably not going to do so now. But that doesn't mean you shouldn't learn this rule, because mastering it will help you get along with others, enjoy true success in all you do, and just be a better person in general. Plus, it's going to make you look very good in God's eyes.

God first set down a list of rules for us to follow a long time ago when he sent a guy named Moses into the desert. Moses was supposed to lead the people of Israel from Egypt to the Promised Land.

If your parents ever take you on a family trip in which you're stuck in the backseat of a car for twelve hours, you'll know that traveling for a long time isn't fun. Moses's trip to the Promised Land was supposed to take about eleven days, but there was so much rebellion and complaining on the part of the people that everything got off schedule, and the trip lasted *forty years*.

While they were traveling, God called Moses up to the top of Mount Sinai, where he spent forty days and forty nights listening to God explain the laws He wanted His people to follow. At the end of the forty days, God gave Moses two stone slabs on which He'd inscribed the Ten Commandments: the rules that the people were supposed to follow if they wanted to lead a godly life.

Moses thought his people would be thrilled to have all the rules outlined in such a simple order. But when he came down from Mount Sinai, he found that the people had gotten out of control while he was gone. They were partying, drinking, and worshipping false gods— not the sorts of things God's chosen people were supposed to be doing. Moses was so ticked off he took the set of tablets and threw them down the mountain at some of the people. This episode just goes to show how badly we humans need laws!

Many years later, Jesus made things even simpler. First, He took those Ten Commandments and condensed them down to two: "Love the Lord your God with all your heart, and love your neighbor as yourself." Wow—*that* was easy. Well, it was at least easy to say. Turned out it was rather difficult for people to actually do either of these things.

Jesus knew the hardest rule for us to follow would be loving other people. I mean, God is perfect so it's easy to love Him, but loving other people can be a real challenge. So Jesus decided to sum up His first two laws into one *big* law that got right to the heart of the matter: "Do unto others as you would have them do unto you." Since doing unto God as we'd want God to do to us is implied by this phrase, these eleven words are really all you need to know to get by.

My own mother laid down this rule for me long before I could have possibly understood how important it was. I mean, I knew I wasn't supposed to hit people or yell at them or put mud in their chocolate milk when they weren't looking, but as I grew up I found that this law was a pretty big deal and covered about everything. My mother called it "the Golden Rule," and as simple as it was, its significance grew as I grew.

Whenever I did something my mother considered borderline delinquent, she popped out the Golden Rule, and told me that I wasn't keeping it. I came to the conclusion that I was a serial Golden Rule violator, because throwing rocks at cars, saying curse words, getting into fights with kids from the neighborhood, and hitting my older sister (even though I'll bet she deserved it sometimes) all went against the Golden Rule.

I spent a great deal of my childhood thinking that the Golden Rule might be a bit too strict to keep. How about a "Silver Rule," or even a "Bronze Rule," or better yet an "Aluminum Rule," which would have had lower standards and would have at least let me say a few bad words, hit the kids in the neighborhood who made fun of me, and occasionally pop my sister just because she was irritating me or I was bored.

I often argued that maybe my parents had misunderstood God. Surely He didn't expect you to let someone call you a name or steal your lunch money without *some* retaliation. Obviously He meant to say, "Do unto others *before* they do unto you" or "Do unto others in the same way they did unto you." After all, wasn't it the God of the Old Testament who said it was okay to take "an eye for an eye" if someone wronged you? I thought my logic was sound, considering these rules actually reflected the way most people behaved, but I got nowhere.

My mother kept repeating the rule to me for years and years until I could repeat it in my sleep. And it eventually paid off because—well into my adulthood—I finally started to understand it. Not only was this rule so simple a child could grasp the concept, but it really does underline every other important rule there is. If everyone followed this rule, we wouldn't need rules against stealing or killing or lying because no one would do those things anyway. They wouldn't do something to someone else that they didn't want someone to do to them.

The problem is, very few people today believe they should have to follow any rules. Instead, most of us think the rules we have should be bent to meet the way we live instead of bending the way we live in order to obey the rules. That's why there is such a big fight over whether we ought to change the rules about which people can marry each other and which people have the right to life.

The odd thing is, the further we've drifted from the simplest rules of "Do unto others as they do unto us" and adopted the less restrictive versions that let us do pretty much what we want, the more we've needed rules to keep everyone in check. The rules grow not only in number, but in complexity, which means different people interpret the rules to mean different things. Then these people sue each other and they bring in a roomful of lawyers to figure out what the rule means. Sometimes even they can't figure it out, so they call in an even bigger, more important lawyer, called a judge, who decides what he thinks the rule should mean. And when it's over, no one is happy except the lawyers who made a lot of money, and everyone seems to know less than when they started.

I'll admit, I'm not as good as my mother was at following the Golden Rule. I lack patience, which means I can get irritated with people easily even when they haven't done anything wrong. This usually happens while I'm standing in the security line at the airport and the person in front of me doesn't seem to realize that water is a liquid. But I certainly try harder than I did when I was little because I understand why the rule is so important. I don't want people lying to me, stealing from me, hitting me, deceiving me, hurting me, betraying me, talking about me behind my back, or ridiculing me. I don't want people to keep me waiting, promise me something they don't deliver, or say they feel something or will do something they don't feel or won't do. And because I don't want anyone doing that to me, I shouldn't do those things to anyone else.

In so many ways, I'm sorry you were born into the world as it is now. Sad to say, your grandparents' generation, the baby boomers, as they have been called, haven't really treated your generation as they would want to be treated. They decided that they wanted to have a lot of things they couldn't afford on their own—like retirement money and health care—and so they made the government borrow a lot of money from other countries knowing full well that their kids and grandkids would eventually have to pay it back. To make matters worse, thanks to a bunch of silly rules, you'll also have to pay some of your hard-earned money (money you made by working hard the way your grandpa taught you) to the government, which will spend it in ways you probably won't like. You'll probably say this isn't fair, which shows how smart you are, but I won't be able to really explain why this happens until you're a little older.

As bad as some of these things seem to you now, they're actually a whole lot better than they used to be. You see, as simple as it should be to treat others as you want to be treated, there was an ugly time in our nation's past when we failed to live up to that standard and, in the process, did a lot of terrible things and hurt a lot of innocent people. And not only did we not live up to the Golden Rule, we also broke the first rule of America, which is stated quite plainly in our Constitution.

This rule says that "all men are created equal" and, therefore, should all be treated the same.

You will grow up realizing that people are different. You'll notice that boys are different from girls—in more ways than you can ever imagine! You'll notice that some people have dark hair, some have light hair, and some have almost no hair. Some people have very light, almost snow-white, skin, while others' skin is more tan or dark brown. Let me let you in on a very important truth: No matter how different people look from you, they are just as important and valuable. You are not better than them, and they are not better than you. God made all of you and He loves you all the same.

In the early years of our wonderful nation, some Americans ignored this rule and engaged in a despicable practice called slavery, in which black men and women from Africa—a continent on the other side of the ocean from us—were kidnapped, separated from their families, and sent to America, where they were forced to work without pay for white people. Slaves were not treated well, often forced to live in shacks and eat low-quality food. If they ever protested, fought back, or tried to run away, they were punished and sometimes killed.

As unthinkably immoral as it was, many Americans justified owning slaves by saying black people were not as good as white people. Slave owners thought they were better than their slaves because they had white skin, better formal education, and more money—three things that certainly made them different, but absolutely not *better* than anyone. Americans were not the first nor the last people to treat others poorly because they were different, and you will probably meet people who think they are better than others. But trust your grandpa when I tell you that, in the eyes of God, no one is better than anyone else. Period.

Luckily, the official practice of slavery ended with the courageous actions of President Abraham Lincoln, who signed the Emancipation Proclamation and set the slaves free. Sadly, though, while a government can change its rules, that doesn't necessarily change people's minds or hearts. Although your grandpa was born more than ninety years after President Lincoln made slavery illegal in this country, I grew up during a time when black people were still treated differently than white people. America may have ended slavery, but it still had a long way to go on the "all men are created equal" idea.

As hard as it might be for you to believe, any black child I grew up with was forced to drink from a different public water fountain and sit in a separate area of a movie theater. He was told to sit in the back of a public bus while the white people sat up front, and if a white person asked for his seat, he was forced to give it up. He was not allowed to eat in the same area of a restaurant or diner as white people and was forced to attend a different school—one where he used old books and equipment that the white schools had thrown away. If he walked into a church that whites attended, he was told to leave. It's hard to fathom how Christians could treat a little child so poorly just because he was black. Clearly they must not have been reading the Bible, otherwise they would know that Jesus said, "Let the little children come to me," and it would be better that a millstone be hanged around the sinners' necks and they were drowned in the depths of the sea than to offend one of these children.

Even though this way of life was normal back then, I knew, even as a child, it was wrong. I remember asking my parents why this was and being told, "It's just the way things are." But it never seemed like the way things *should* be. Finally, the courts—which do occasionally get rid of bad rules—decreed that things had to change. But that didn't mean change was easy or immediate. In 1954 (a year before I was born), the Supreme Court—the most powerful court in our country—declared that schools had to offer equal opportunities for education regardless of race. But I was in the fifth grade before I met my first black classmate. Her name was Beverly, and looking back, I realize how brave this little ten-year-old girl must have been. Many of my classmates were polite and treated her with respect, but some called her names and treated her badly. Later on I realized that Beverly's parents must have been just as courageous, because they surely knew just how difficult it would be for their little girl to attend a school where everyone else was white. I didn't know Beverly's parents, but I'd guess they sent their daughter to a white school because they knew it would help make things easier for all the kids who came after Beverly, that the more black children were sent to white schools, the less children would pay attention to the differences that had once separated them.

When I went to the sixth grade, three other black children joined our class, and in the ninth grade the previously all-black school in our town completely merged with the white school. Change was happening fast, but plenty of people clung to their old attitudes and prejudices. One of the biggest turning points happened in September 1957, when nine black children tried to enroll at Little Rock Central High School in Little Rock, Arkansas. Although under the law they had every right to attend the school, the governor of Arkansas stood in the doorway and denied them admission. Only when President Dwight D. Eisenhower intervened and sent federal troops down south to protect the students were they able to enter.

Exactly forty years later, on a September morning in 1997, your grandpa stood with President Bill Clinton and Mayor Jim Dailey of Little Rock and held open the door of Little Rock Central to those same nine students. Of course, by then they were in their late fifties and I was the forty-fourth governor of the state, but so much else had changed. Opening the door for them was one of the most memorable and emotional moments of my life.

Scarlett, what made that day even more special was that your mother was a student at Little Rock Central by then. Just days before, I had picked her up from school, along with one of her good friends, Jessica, a young lady who happened to be black. As the two girls piled into the backseat of the car and I drove them to the governor's mansion so they could study together for the afternoon, I knew your mother couldn't possibly realize how much had changed in those forty years. She and her friend did not consider each other different at all. They were just two fifteen-year-old girls who became good friends and went to the same school. The fact that one was white and one was black didn't matter. Nor did the fact that one was the governor's daughter. They were equals.

Chandler and Scarlett, I love you both so much, and there aren't many ways you could ever break my heart. But one way would be if you ever treated someone with disrespect. To me you are about the most special people in the whole world, but that doesn't mean you are more special to God than anyone else. And if God doesn't have the right to treat people differently, then you certainly don't.

As I tried to tell you earlier, you aren't but two generations removed from living in a house without electricity or covered floors. Your parents, grandparents, and great-grandparents all worked very hard so you'd have opportunities beyond any we once could have dreamed of. But that doesn't mean you have the right to treat people with less money, education, or opportunities as less worthy of those things than you. In fact, it is your responsibility as someone who has been blessed to treat those less fortunate with kindness.

Your grandpa was once a governor and ran for president, but every day I remember where I came from. I was always more comfortable around the people who worked in the kitchen than those who sat at the head table, anyway. Heck, I already knew how to work in the kitchen, but I had to learn how to sit at the head table! But even when I do get asked to sit at the head table, I've never forgotten the person who fills up my glass, serves my dinner, or cleans up the room after everyone leaves. In fact, I always try to be generous to servers in restaurants. When your uncle John Mark was in high school, he spent some time working in food service, and I never forgot the stories he told of people who treated him like a robot, demanded the most attention, and then failed to reward his service with a decent tip. There are times when I see a particularly harried server who is on her feet all day, taking orders, rushing to get people what they want when they want it, and I realize that this person is probably working very hard to take care of children, pay rent, put gas in the car and groceries on the table. I will sometimes leave a tip far beyond the cost of the meal because I know the person I'm giving it to will probably appreciate it more than I do.

Once I left a hundred-dollar tip at a restaurant at the Atlanta airport during a busy lunchtime because the server was working hard, trying to be pleasant, and taking care of her customers with a cheerful attitude. I quietly added the tip to my credit card receipt, and was walking out when she came to me as I approached the exit. There were tears in her eyes as she tracked me down to say, "Thank you so much! I needed that today." I don't think it was just the money she needed. She needed to be told that she mattered and that her work was valued.

I'm not always going to be around to make sure you follow the Golden Rule, and I know there will be times when you're really not going to want to. Someday, someone will be mean to you. (I sure hope I'm not around that day because they'll have me to deal with!) Try not to get angry or get even. You don't want to be "even" with someone who acts like that. Think about how it makes you feel and how much it hurts for some-one to be mean and spiteful toward you. Reflect upon how painful it is that someone tried to humiliate you or looked down on you. And then promise God, your grandpa, and yourself that you will never purposely make someone else feel like that. Go out of your way to be nice to people, especially the ones others ignore and mistreat. Just treat others as you want them to treat you. If you do that, you'll see that the Golden Rule is a pretty good rule after all.

CHAPTER SIX

On Pets

Dear Chandler, Dear Scarlett:

One of the greatest joys and one of the greatest pains you will ever experience is owning pets. My guess is that you'll have dogs around pretty much all the time because we are a dog family. Nothing against cats, rabbits, hamsters, fish, birds, chickens, horses, or even pigs—they make great pets for other people. I've even heard of people who keep raccoons as pets, but for the life of me I can't imagine why. Your parents have tried other pets along the way, but in my opinion a good dog may be the greatest animal God ever made. In some cases they're more pleasant to be around than people.

There's a lot to be learned from any pet, but dogs are in a league to themselves as far as I'm concerned. No matter what, a dog always loves you. A dog is loyal, and when every last friend you have quits on you, he will still crawl up in your lap like you're the greatest thing on earth.

President Harry Truman once gave great advice to politicians everywhere: "If you want a friend in Washington, get a dog." Having been in politics and having owned dogs, this makes perfect sense to me. Dogs don't read editorial pages or blogs. They never pay attention to attack ads on radio or TV, and they sleep through most of the talking-head news shows so they don't hear, much less believe, the snarky stuff people say about you. Dogs will always keep a secret and they will never lie to you or steal from you. They don't ask for special favors other than a dog treat now and then, and even if they don't get it, they don't go off and bite you. People do! A dog's expectations are pretty straightforward: Give him food, water, and a little attention and he'll follow you to the ends of the earth and beyond. They never fight with you and they don't care about wearing the latest fashions. In fact, most dogs hate wearing anything other than the fur God gave them. They hear better than you ever will, smell things you can't even notice, and sense danger long before you do. A dog may even save your life someday.

Another former president, Woodrow Wilson, said, "If a dog will not come to you after having looked you in the face, you should go home and examine your conscience." It's true: If your dog doesn't like someone, you probably shouldn't, either. I have found that my dogs are usually better judges of someone's character than I am. People tend to believe the best in others even if their gut tells them not to. Dogs don't. If they get a bad feeling, they will let you know.

Your grandpa has had dogs since he was a little boy. My first was a little mutt called Moochy, which we named after a character in a Walt Disney movie—I don't remember which one, because I was too little. In fact, I don't remember much about Moochy at all other than that he was black and white and very little. I never really knew what happened to Moochy, but he disappeared from our lives sometime when I was about four.

By the time I got to be about eight or nine years old, I really wanted another dog. My mother didn't want us to get one because she didn't think my sister and I would take care of him, and it was already a big enough struggle for our parents to feed two growing children, let alone a growing dog. I'm not sure if it was because of my persistent begging or because my dad was a huge softy, but somehow we came home one day from my uncle Alvin's house with one of the eight puppies his dog Jessie had just had. Uncle Alvin had pretended he was doing us a big favor by giving us one of the puppies, but the older I got, the more I realized that we were the ones doing *him* a big favor by taking one of those puppies off his hands.

But I was sure glad we got that little dog. He was a dachshund mix and I named him Cosmo. The space program was in full swing at the time, and pretty much every little boy in America dreamed of being an astronaut. Cosmo seemed like the perfect name for a little brown dog with long floppy ears and boundless energy. For the next nine years, Cosmo was as much a part of our family as I was. Sometimes I thought my parents might like him more than me because he certainly got into a whole lot less trouble than I did!

Cosmo was with us before the days of leash laws, so he could run around wherever he wanted, but he never ran off. I don't blame him. He had it pretty good. My dad built him a little white doghouse with a shingled roof and he always had fresh water and food. My mother pretended as though she never liked Cosmo, but my sister and I would sometimes catch her talking to him and petting him. She loved him just as much as the rest of us. And then one day, Cosmo disappeared.

We looked everywhere for him, all day and well into the night. We asked all the neighbors if they had seen him, and we even put a little ad in the local newspaper for a lost dog. Nothing. Each morning I'd go looking for Cosmo until it was time to go to school, and in the afternoon I'd ride my bicycle all over town trying to find him. Even my mother looked for him.

The time came when we finally had to accept that Cosmo wasn't coming back. We never found out if he got hit by a car, picked up by a dognapper, or just got sick and went off to die. I would finish junior high and high school, go off to college, get married, and have my own kids before I'd have another dog. Not because I didn't want one, but because I wasn't sure I could handle the pain of losing another one.

I didn't think about getting another dog until one day, when your parents were little, I got a call from my friend John Lile, a prominent attorney in our town of Pine Bluff, Arkansas. Chandler, your dad was about four years old, and, Scarlett, your mother was only two when John called and said, "Your kids need a dog and I have a litter of puppies. I'll give you one." I tried to convince John and myself that my kids weren't old enough to take care of a dog and that we didn't have the time to take care of one properly. John insisted, and your parents and Uncle John Mark begged us to take one of the dogs. Despite my reservations about bringing into my life another dog that might die or disappear, I, like most parents, gave in.

The dog we brought home from the Liles was a beautiful and graceful English setter puppy that showed up with the energy of a nuclear weapon and the most gentle spirit we could have hoped for. He looked at us as if he knew he was supposed to be part of our family, and those big eyes won my heart from the moment I saw him. As much as I had tried to steel myself against being emotional about another dog, I couldn't help but feel a childlike joy inside. He had a white coat with black markings and some black fur around his eyes that made him look like he was wearing a mask. It reminded us of the Lone Ranger (a reference I hope you'll understand one day), so we named him Ranger.

There was nothing anyone could do to make that dog mad. Sarah was only two, so she didn't always know that she wasn't supposed to pull on his ears or try to ride him like a pony, but whenever she did, he never showed any sign of displeasure.

Although he was a good dog and we took good care of him, Ranger wasn't without his share of adventures. One day, Ranger ran off somewhere and didn't come home. We searched for two days but couldn't find him, and I was worried he might have suffered the same fate as Cosmo. He had tags, so we assumed that if he'd been picked up someone would call us, but we decided to go to the pound anyway in case he had lost his tags. The entire family decided to go and when we arrived, we asked if animal control had picked up any dogs that met the description of Ranger. They said no. We asked if we could look around anyway, but we didn't see him. Discouraged, we figured we'd never see Ranger again and decided to go home.

As we were leaving, David called out Ranger's name real loud, just to be sure. We immediately heard the familiar bark that we knew could only be Ranger. He had been placed in another part of the pound where animal control was getting ready to put him down. I think we all cried—first out of happiness that we'd found him but also because we knew what his fate would have been had we not arrived just in the nick of time.

It turned out animal control had picked Ranger up at the airport near our house, where he'd been caught chasing airplanes down the runway. You see, Ranger was bred to be a bird-hunting dog, so it was in his blood to chase things that flew. I suppose he thought the planes were just really large birds!

He hadn't lost his tags after all, and I've never understood why the people at the animal shelter told us they didn't have a dog like him. I'm not sure if they were just too busy or just didn't care, but I believe the only people who should be able to decide when a dog is put to sleep should be those who love him, not those who've found him.

Ranger made me cry only one other time. By the time he was fifteen years old, we were living in the governor's mansion, where he had nearly nine acres on which to frolic and play and a large staff of workers to pet, feed, and play with him twenty-four hours a day. He loved it there, and why wouldn't he?

But as he got older, he got frailer and could barely move around. We took him to the vet several times, but one afternoon when your grandmother and I went to pick him up from another visit to Dr. Paladino's office, he couldn't come to us when he heard us calling. He tried to get up but was so weak he fell on the floor. The vet told us he was in pain and couldn't hold on much longer. We couldn't bear to see him suffer, so we made the tough decision to allow Dr. Paladino to put him down. He told us we could leave the room while it happened, but there was no way I was going to abandon Ranger in his last minutes on this earth. He had been part of our family for fifteen years and had never failed to provide his unconditional love and companionship. The thought of leaving him on a cold table to die alone never crossed my mind. So as tears streamed down my face, your grandmother and I held Ranger in our arms as he quietly breathed his last breath. David was with us, too, and on the way home, we all cried.

Afterward, your grandmother made a little casket from wood, I dug a grave in the backyard of the governor's mansion, and we buried Ranger and placed a nice tombstone on his grave that I suppose is still there to this day. We laid him next to President Clinton's dog Zeke, which had died while he was governor, and a cat that had belonged to Jim Guy Tucker, the governor who had preceded me.

Once again, the loss of a pet had broken my heart and made me think I'd never want another one. Not that I didn't love every minute they were around, but I knew they wouldn't be around forever and I didn't want to feel that pain ever again.

Your parents tried other pets from time to time. David once had a cockatiel that he named Scrub, which was David's nickname because he was always kind of "scrubby." David thought he could teach the cockatiel to talk, so he made a tape that repeated "Hello, Scrub" over and over. I think it would have been easier to get peace in the Middle East than to get that bird to talk!

Sarah had a fish, a turtle, and a chicken, and she even brought a cat home once. Ranger chased the cat up a tree and it took hours to get it down. We decided that a cat probably wasn't going to work. We tried a lot of various pets, but none of them were like dogs.

After Ranger died, I was pretty sure I couldn't handle another dog. Not only was the pain of losing them too great, but I had a state to run and didn't think I could handle the responsibility. Your grandmother had other ideas.

On a day in late May of 1998, about a year after Ranger died, I was attending a parade and festival in Mena, Arkansas, with your grandmother. It was right around our twenty-fourth wedding anniversary, and I was speaking at a luncheon crowd after having ridden in the parade earlier. In the middle of my speech, your grandmother did something that made me think she'd lost her mind. She stood up and said, "I need to see you a minute!" I'll admit, your grandmother has done some things that have surprised me, but nothing quite like that! I paused and looked at her and she said it again—out loud—in front of a couple hundred people. "I need for you to come with me a minute. It's very important."

With that, I turned the microphone over to the master of ceremonies and excused myself. I followed your grandmother out of the event center, and when we got outside, I saw a small portable dog pen containing several Labrador retriever puppies, all running around. "Happy anniversary!" she said. "Pick out a puppy!" She explained that she'd had to interrupt my speech because the puppies were about to overwhelm the breeder, but the event organizers had been in on the plan as well.

If I have learned one thing in my now more than thirty-eight years of marriage, it's not to argue with your grandmother or try to return a gift she gives you. So here I stood looking into a portable pen of little Lab puppies, all of which were jumping around and being, well, puppies. Then one caught my eye. He was jet black and even though he was playful like the rest, he seemed to have a presence about him. He had poise for a puppy, and he seemed to be looking right at me. It was an easy pick. "I'll take that little black one."

It turned out the breeder from whom Janet had bought the puppy had been the same breeder from whom our friends Frank and Cathy Keating, the governor and first lady of Oklahoma, had gotten their Lab, Tazzie. Cathy and your grandmother had conspired with each other to set up this surprise, and when I pointed out the pup I wanted, the breeder said, "That's the pick of the litter. It's the one I would have chosen, too."

From the moment I picked up that cuddly little Lab pup with his big black feet and big brown eyes, we bonded in a way that I can't quite describe. I went back in to finish my speech with him still nestled between my elbow and wrist. Of course, I first had to explain that Janet had interrupted my speech because she had surprised me with a pen full of little jumping puppies for our anniversary. I held my new friend through the rest of the speech and all the way to the airport for the one-hour flight back to Little Rock. The dog literally didn't leave my arms until we arrived at the governor's mansion that afternoon.

We named him Jet because not only was his coat jet black, but the first hour I had him we flew together on a prop-jet airplane. Plus, he was fast like a jet, with strong, muscular legs and a will to win at whatever he did. Jet was my best friend. On many days, when the task of being governor had taken its toll on me, he seemed like my only friend. Maybe it was because we needed each other, or maybe it was because he hung around me whenever I was home, but we were virtually inseparable. He was my hunting and fishing buddy, and if he saw me wearing camo gear, he would run around in circles and dance around the room knowing that he was going hunting. I loved hunting before I met Jet, but I always had more fun with him there.

The staff at the governor's office all joked that if they were ever reincarnated, they wanted to come back as Jet. As the "first dog" of Arkansas, Jet did have it pretty good. It helped that he has always been well behaved—especially for a dog with that much energy. In the house, he is calm, never gets into things, or tears things up the way some Labs do. When I was governor, he was present at all my meetings and press conferences, where he would usually curl up right in front of my feet.

As much as I loved Cosmo and Ranger, Jet is a canine pal like no other. Maybe because the stress of being governor just made him more valuable as a constant companion, but in my 2002 reelection campaign, when we traveled the state for months in a large RV, Jet lived on board with me the entire time. My staff agreed that Jet kept my blood pressure down and kept me utterly at peace even when things got really stressful. There were times during the campaign when a reporter would get especially testy with me at an event and try to ambush me with "gotcha" questions. I often got stressed and angry at those moments, but when I stepped into the campaign RV and Jet crawled up in my lap, I felt my emotional temperature go back to normal.

I believe that pets (especially dogs) make us better humans. They love us when no one else seems to. They read our moods and react to them. Even though Jet was more "my dog," and the bond between us was ironclad, there were moments when his instincts were simply remarkable. He usually slept on the floor next to my side of the bed, but he loved everyone in the family. Once, Janet had to have surgery and when I brought her home and put her in bed, Jet did something he'd never done before. Instead of taking his normal place beside me, he very gently went to Janet's side of the bed and for the next three nights as she recuperated, he stayed by her side constantly, as if keeping vigil until she felt better. Even spouses have a hard time doing that!

As your parents grew up and went off to college and started their own families and careers, your grandmother and I added two other dogs to our family. Sonic, the little black shih tzu, was named after your grandmother's favorite fast-food place, the Sonic drive-in. He was so tiny when I got him for her for Christmas in 2005, I actually presented him to her in a Sonic soda cup. If I thought one dog was enough, two certainly kept life interesting, especially because Jet was a seventy-five-pound Lab and Sonic was a tiny ten-pound sack of fur that always believed he was the big dog.

In early 2007, while I was away from home running for president, your grandmother called to say, "We have another boy." Without telling me, she had brought home a little Cavalier King Charles spaniel puppy because she saw him and couldn't resist. I was adamant. "We already have two dogs and are barely able to take care of them due to the campaign schedule and my crazy travel," I protested. "We most certainly cannot and will not have a third dog!" I told her that, as soon as I got home later that week, I'd help her find another good home for the new puppy.

But when I came home that weekend, the little pup jumped up in my lap, looked right into my face with his big brown eyes, and licked me real good. At that moment I knew there was no way we were giving up that little dog. And that's how Toby (named after my bass guitar, a Tobias), became part of the family.

Your parents and Uncle John Mark think we ended up with three dogs because we were trying to make up for the fact that our three kids had left home and we needed something else to take care of. They even complained we treated the dogs better than we ever treated them. Of course, we reminded them, the dogs behaved better than they did, too!

As I write these pages, Sonic and Toby are still full of mischief, but Jet is fourteen years old—far older than most Labs live to be. I know Jet can't live forever, but in a way he will. As will Cosmo and Ranger, and Sonic, and Toby. They will live in my heart and memory as some of the greatest joys I've known in life. When I'm on the road and away, I call to check on them. I miss them and can't wait to get home to have them jump in my lap and show me how glad they are I'm home. They are worth every penny I spend on their food, their medical care, and their toys, because when it seems as if my world has fallen apart, they help God put it back together again.

And, Chandler and Scarlett, that is exactly why you need to have pets. Not because I want you to experience the pain of losing them, but because they will bring you so much joy while they're around. Sure, you could spend your time doing things that are much more fun than feeding or cleaning up after a pet and that won't cause you as much heartbreak later on. And, sure, you have plenty of other people around you—like your parents and grandparents—who will love you more than any dog can. But I want you to experience the love and joy only a great pet—especially a great dog—can bring. Sure, it will hurt when they die—it always hurts when something or someone you love leaves—but you'll get to see them again because I'm pretty sure there are dogs in heaven. I'm sometimes not sure I'd want to go if there weren't.

CHAPTER SEVEN

On America

Dear Chandler, Dear Scarlett:

It will be a long time before you fully understand how fortunate you are to be little Americans. For now let me say that you live in one of the only countries on earth where one of the biggest ongoing political fights is not over how to keep people from escaping the country, but how to deal with the millions who keep trying to get in. So you should never take it for granted that you are already here.

When you get older, you will probably hear about and hopefully even listen to the music of a group called U2. Their lead singer is a man named Bono (no, that's not his real name, but if you ever meet him, that's what you should call him). After becoming a big rock star, Bono founded an organization called the ONE campaign, which helps combat hunger, poverty, and disease in Third World countries. You grandpa once traveled to Rwanda for ONE, and, Scarlett, your mother once worked for ONE as the campaign manager for the 2012 election cycle.

Bono is an Irishman who has traveled the entire world. Yet in a visit with me, he said something about America that I'll never forget. He said that while he certainly loves his native Ireland (I took your parents there once, and it is a beautiful and hospitable country), he admires America because it is not just a "country, but an idea."

I think Bono's comment is a beautiful assessment of our homeland, especially coming from a worldly and very famous foreigner. What Bono meant was that America is unique because people can come here from all cultures, languages, races, religions, and countries and live the rest of their lives in freedom. I only wish every American could appreciate the unique and exceptional blessings that our visitors seem to understand.

In the great scheme of things, America is a pretty young country. Some nations have been around for centuries, but the United States was officially born in 1776, making it less than 250 years old. Compared to England, France, Italy, China, or many other nations, we're a child. But in that relatively short period of time, we have grown from being a pioneer place on the outer limits of the world's frontier to being the most powerful and prosperous land in the history of civilization.

The people who set the stage for those who would eventually go on to found our government were the Pilgrims. They were mostly Europeans who had been persecuted in their home countries for belonging to a specific religion and therefore had fled in search of a place where they could worship freely. Back then, many countries were governed by a rigid class system in which people of a certain wealth, religion, or ethnicity were given more rights and opportunities than others. Under this system, a person's station in life was pretty much determined by the family and economic class into which he or she was born. There was little "mobility into nobility" and those born poor were destined to remain poor, while those born into privilege were given every freedom they could possibly enjoy.

Many years later, when our Founding Fathers decided to form a new government, they remembered the plight of their predecessors and decreed that no one is born better than anyone else. "We hold these truths to be self-evident," they wrote in the Declaration of Independence, "that all men are created equal, that they are endowed by their Creator with certain unalienable Rights, that among these are Life, Liberty and the pursuit of Happiness."

There's so much in that one phrase that it's hard to take it all in. To say that "all men are created equal" was a fundamentally unique and radical idea because no other country treated its citizens equally. And to say that the "truths are self-evident" was to assert that not only was the statement true, but that it was so obviously true it shouldn't even need to be explained. Basically, we were telling the rest of the world that they'd governed the wrong way for centuries, but America had figured it out.

Today we hear these words so often that we tend to not give them much thought. Chandler and Scarlett, had it not been for those words and the blood that was shed to enshrine them into law, you most certainly would not be enjoying much of what you enjoy today. I told you earlier that while your ancestry isn't something to be heralded in the history books, neither is it something to be ashamed of. You come from a long line of people who started poor and who, because of where they lived and the amount of education they had, never knew much beyond a life of hard work and hard times. But thanks to our founders, they were treated as equals before the law and therefore given the opportunity to go to school so they could get better jobs and advance, generation after generation.

Unfortunately, even though we established this incredible expression of equality, it wasn't always fully followed. Women were certainly not treated as equals to men. They weren't allowed to go to certain schools or work certain jobs and, until 1920, they weren't even allowed to vote. Scarlett, it's a good thing you weren't born a hundred years ago, because if you're anything like your mother you probably wouldn't be too happy not getting to vote or be involved in political activities.

And as I mentioned earlier, people of color were actually considered property, not people, and were "owned" as slaves and treated worse than animals. How could this have happened in a society that says "all men are created equal"? Good question. And the answer is terrible. The reason Americans let themselves get away with this for so long was because they didn't define black people as real people, but as inferior beings. Fortunately, people who did have the right to vote eventually realized this was wrong and began demanding that black people be considered citizens. Once they gained this recognition, they began to demand more and more rights and, slowly but surely, were granted protections that were once thought impossible. In America, power does not rest with one all-powerful person who makes up his own rules; it rests in the hands of the people, who can fight for what they believe in and actually effect change.

Unfortunately, there are still people in this country who aren't considered to be real people: unborn children. I have been fighting to change this since I was in college because I believe it is as important as standing against the evils of racism. Some people say that because an unborn child can't walk or talk or care for itself, it is not a person. By that logic, anyone who cannot take care of himself shouldn't be considered a person, either, but there are plenty of Americans who struggle with mental or physical disabilities and receive care and support from the government. So why not our most defenseless citizens? My hope is that you will live to see the day when we value people before they are born as well as after and that you will know an America that doesn't treat a baby as expendable, disposable, or lacking in value.

Your country has made its share of mistakes. It is far from a perfect nation, and we will always struggle with our frailties and failures. But the best part about living in America is that the people have the power to change things. When we decide laws are wrong, we can change them. If we decide our Constitution could use some more explanation or clarity, we can amend it. And if we decide the people we elected to run our cities, states, and nation aren't doing a good job, we can change them, too. In many other countries, a change of government comes at the end of a gun barrel, and bullets and bombs instead of ballots are the means by which people get what they want.

You will sometimes hear people talk about how "ugly" our elections can be, and someday I'll sit you down and tell you all the ugly stories from my experience in politics. But, trust me, I'd rather live in a place where people are free to criticize and ridicule one another—even me—than a place where anyone who so much as questions the government can end up in jail or dead.

You should never take this freedom for granted. Your country did not become what it is because some smart people had some nice thoughts that they decided to write down. Ever since our Founding Fathers wrote their famous words in the Declaration of Independence, others have been trying to destroy their idea, and the brave men and women of our military have fought and died to protect it. You might choose to serve in the military someday, and if you do, you will be among the few true heroes in our nation.

I was a teenager during the Vietnam War, which was a very controversial and unpopular war that many people—including many Americans—protested. There weren't enough soldiers who volunteered to serve in this war, so the government instituted something called the draft, which meant that any man over the age of eighteen could be called to serve unless he had a medical problem or some other reason he couldn't fight.

By the time I turned eighteen, in August of 1973, the draft had ended and the war was coming to an end, so the military wasn't looking for many new recruits.

When I went to college, I became part of ROTC (Reserve Officers' Training Corps), which had been mandatory at Ouachita Baptist University for decades. It wasn't too long into my freshman year when the colonel who ran the program told me he really didn't need me to stay in ROTC anymore. He said that, given my extremely flat feet, the army wouldn't take me even if I begged to join, and he didn't see any reason for me to continue. There have been times when I wished I had served, but that was the closest I came. Since then, however, my respect and gratitude for those who do wear the uniform has only deepened.

Chandler and Scarlett, things are pretty good for you right now. There is no war being fought on American soil, and you are a long way from having to decide whether or not you want to go into the military. But whether or not you decide to serve, I hope you will never take your freedom for granted. I hope you will vote in every election, donate money to causes you support, and fight to protect your right to life, liberty, and the pursuit of happiness. When you say your bedtime prayers every night, you should always thank God for your mommy and daddy and of course for your grandpa. But you should also thank Him for the United States of America.

CHAPTER EIGHT

On Love and Marriage

Dear Chandler, Dear Scarlett:

I hope you are always nice and respectful to everyone you meet, but when it comes to dealing with people of the opposite sex, there are a few specific things you need to know. For one, you will treat members of the opposite sex differently throughout different phases of your life. Right now and for the next few years, gender won't matter much to you. You will be aware that boys look different from girls and that they might like to do different things or play with different kinds of toys. But you'll probably have friends who are boys and friends who are girls and not think a thing about it.

Then, when you are five or six years old, you will start to pay more attention to the differences between boys and girls. Most likely you'll see a baby getting a diaper changed, and you'll ask why what your parents call your "private parts" are different from theirs. Your parents probably won't give you a good answer because, well, it's complicated. Later on, when you finally find out the reason, you'll understand why they didn't want to tell you.

Don't feel like you're missing out on key information, though. Pretty much all parents give their kids the same goofy and incomplete answers that parents have been giving for thousands of years. I know this because I did the same thing when Chandler's dad and Scarlett's mom started asking me those questions. And I'd do the same for you, too. Your parents might try to bring you to my house one day and get me to answer your questions for them, but I think I'll decline that opportunity. I'll insist that your parents, who always acted like they knew so much more than I did when they were children, have the pleasure of giving you the full details.

Once you start learning just how different boys and girls are, you'll probably decide you don't care much for the other gender. Boys will group with boys and girls with girls, and they'll probably pick on each other. Boys will call girls "icky" and girls will say the boys have "cooties."

Scarlett, you probably won't want to hang out with boys anyway, because at that age they'll be too busy seeing how long they can go without a bath, carrying lizards and frogs in their pockets, and doing really dumb things on their bicycles and skateboards to prove how tough they are.

And, Chandler, don't fret if girls stand in a little group with their hands over their mouths looking, pointing, and giggling in your direction. It doesn't mean anything. Later on, when the girls are in their teens, twenties, or thirties, they will gather in little groups with their hands over their mouths, looking, pointing, and giggling in your direction because they think you're cute. When they reach their forties or fifties, however, they only gather to giggle and point if you've forgotten to zip your pants or you have something in your teeth. *That's* when you should pay attention!

Right before you become a teenager, a day will come when those little girls or little boys you thought were so icky before will start to seem quite wonderful. This isn't because they've become more like you; they've actually become even more different. You'll notice changes in the way they look, the way they smell, the way they act, and the way they act toward *you*. Watch out, kids! Life will never be the same. And you're going to love it!

But just because you'll be more interested in the opposite sex doesn't mean you're going to understand them. Ever since Adam and Eve, men and women have been trying to figure each other out. Books, movies, seminars, TV specials, college courses, and stadium rallies have all been devoted to the effort of solving the great mystery of why men are like men and women are like women. No one has cracked the code. I certainly haven't, and I doubt you will, either. Save yourself some energy: Don't try to blow out the flame of the sun with your breath and don't try to figure out the opposite gender. Just assume that God designed us so very differently from one another and yet made us wildly attracted to one another because He has a sense of humor.

You will probably know many loves in your life. Some you may later decide were just fleeting attractions, but others will always linger in your heart. Memories of these loves will probably make you laugh or smile when you are lonely or in doubt, or they may make you cry—for so many reasons.

But in the midst of all these giddy, highly charged emotional attractions, you will hopefully meet the person who will become your partner for life. And your heart will settle into a feeling much deeper and more immovable than anything you felt before. When the time is right, you will ask this person to marry you so you can spend the rest of your lives together. Next to your decision to give your life and trust to God, the decision you make to marry someone is the biggest and most important in your life. Sure, you will make a lot of important decisions—where to go to college, what job to take, where to live—but if you change your mind about any of these, you can always change colleges or jobs or cities. Marrying someone affects your future in so many more profound ways. It determines what you can do and how you can live and even what your kids are going to look like! Even if the marriage doesn't last (though I pray it will), you will still have to live with the consequences of having married someone in the first place. That's why you need to try to get it right the first time.

Preparing to spend the rest of your life with someone doesn't start when you ask him or her to marry you. Nor does it start when you meet the person for the first time. It actually starts right now, when you're still crawling around the floor as an infant. That's because your views and values regarding the opposite sex are already being shaped by how your parents treat each other.

Chandler and Scarlett, you know how much I love your dad and mom, but I'm also really happy about whom they married. Chandler's mom, Lauren, and Scarlett's dad, Bryan, are wonderful people. Even if we lived in a culture where parents arrange the marriage of their sons and daughters, and even if I had spared no expense or time in scouring the planet to find the perfect spouses for my children, I could not have done as well as they did. I love Lauren and Bryan as if they were my own, and every day I thank God my children were blessed with truly remarkable and wonderful spouses.

I have been blessed to have been married to your grandmother Janet for over thirty-eight years. We've known each other since we were in elementary school and started dating when we were seniors in high school. Our first date was after one of your grandmother's basketball games. She was a star basketball player for the Hope High School Ladycats, and I was broadcasting the play-by-play of the game for KXAR radio, the "voice of Southwest Arkansas." I had hoped to take Janet to dinner, but by the time the game was over, pretty much every restaurant in our tiny town had closed. We ended up at the Fulton truck stop on Interstate 30. It was January 29, 1973. I still remember the date. Heck, I even remember that we ordered chicken fried steak!

Of course, there was no way we could have known our first date at a truck stop after a high school basketball game would be the first of many special times we would spend together. At the time, it was just a simple date between two friends. We had been out together with our friends many times before, but this was the first time we went out alone. In many ways, we were opposites. She was the freewheeling and daring extrovert who liked to take chances and do unconventional things like walk across a suspended pipeline over the Red River. I was more cautious and deliberate in what I did and said. Nevertheless, there was something from that first date that attracted us to each other—and I don't think it was the chicken fried steak!

Janet and I continued to date and our friendship gradually turned into the love that we've now shared for many years. We married after our freshman year in college, a couple of months shy of our nineteenth birthdays. I know Janet didn't marry me for my money, because when I proposed, I had so little money that I couldn't afford a proper engagement ring. So I gave her a toy ring from a gum machine instead. Of course, I promised her a real one was coming—and, believe me, considering the jewelry I've bought for your grandmother since then, I've more than made up for it!

One thing we've learned is that it's easy to get married, but it takes real work to stay married. Love is far more than the emotional giddiness one feels at the beginning of a new romance. Love is the commitment to faithfully act in a loving way toward each other. To do that requires putting the needs of the other above your own. Easier said than done, but the degree to which you do that will determine how successful your marriage is.

Take my advice: Try to get things right the first time. We were young, but we entered into marriage with an understanding that divorce would never be an option for resolving our conflicts. I think it was the smartest decision we ever made. There is no such thing as a perfect marriage, because there are no perfect people—let alone two. But the real joy in a marriage is in knowing that someone will love you in spite of all your faults. Your grandmother has certainly found a few faults in me, but, amazingly, she's stayed around all these years. And I sure am glad, because without her, I wouldn't have the two of you!

Long before you even think about dating and certainly years before you would even be legally old enough to marry, you should start planning for your future. How? The best way is to watch your parents.

Chandler, as you grow up, you need to learn how to respect your mother and treat her like the very special lady that she is. How you treat her will affect how you will treat your own wife one day. And, Scarlett, you need to grow up listening to and learning from your dad and noticing not only all the ways he provides for you, but all the sacrifices he makes in order to protect you and your mom. What you observe now will influence how you treat your own husband and will teach you what a good man does for his family. I don't expect you to fully understand all of this right now, but hopefully you will take my words to heart so you can comprehend them one day.

Another way to prepare for marriage is to start praying for the person who will become your spouse. That boy or girl is probably already born. He or she might live near you or halfway around the world, but your prayers will reach them regardless. Your grandmother was told when she was a little girl that she should start praying for her future husband, and look how incredibly well that worked out! Pray your future spouse has parents who will instill in him or her a strong moral character and an intense awareness of accountability. Pray that they will not make foolish and irrevocable decisions to engage in risky behavior with drugs or alcohol. And pray that they will live a God-centered life.

Chandler, there will certainly come a time when you are long past thinking girls are "icky" and, Scarlett, you will start paying attention to boys when they no longer think it's cool to carry a frog in their pocket. You'll know when that "magic" happens, and when it leads to a decision for you to spend your lives together in marriage, I hope I'm still around to be there.

Our culture glorifies the emotional side of marriage—the courtship, romance, and the . . . other things I'll let your parents tell you about. As a result, if you ask most people why they decided to marry their spouse, they would probably say, "Because she makes me so happy!" But let me tell you a little secret: Great marriages have very little to do with happiness. Allow me to explain.

The word "happy" shares a root with the word "happenstance," which means something that happens by chance. The weather, illness, rejection—all of these things are outside of our control. Do you really want your feelings about the person you spend the rest of your life with to be as fleeting as the weather? I doubt it. The real purpose of marriage is *not* to make you "happy." It's to teach you how to really love someone.

Most people say they *really* love someone before they decide to marry them. This makes sense. Otherwise, why go through all the trouble of planning and paying for a big wedding and inviting all the relatives you don't really like? You wouldn't do that for just *anyone*. There are actually three kinds of love, all of which are involved in marriage, but the most important one does not come naturally to us and takes a lifetime to understand.

The first kind of love is *eros*, which is a Greek word for the very natural urges that occur between men and women. Eros is the kind of love you feel when you enter puberty and realize just how attractive the opposite sex can be. Eros is an important part of a relationship, but it's also the most superficial and least fulfilling part. If you think you love someone just because he or she is "hot," remember that looks can change or diminish over time, as can your feelings for that person. Marriages that are based entirely on eros are pretty shallow, and if all you care about is the way someone looks, you're better off just watching television; there are plenty of hot people there that you don't have to live with.

The second kind of love was also named by the Greeks: *phileo*. Phileo is the love of reciprocity or the love that says, "I will do for you what you do for me." Phileo is sometimes called "brotherly love," and the city of Philadelphia is named for this idea (though, based on how Philadelphians act, you'd never know it!). Phileo is based on the notion that we should give what we get. If someone is kind, we'll be kind; if they are generous, we'll be generous; if they invite us to dinner, we will invite them to dinner. Phileo is a great idea, and very similar to the Golden Rule I told you about earlier. But if it's the best type of love present in a marriage, the result is always disappointing. That's because it's a type of love that keeps score, and since marriage is not like a baseball game where everyone agrees about who is in the lead, keeping score can result in anger, bitterness, and resentment.

We all have expectations. If those expectations go unmet, we become disappointed, which makes us unhappy. If I promise to take you to a ball game, and I don't, I'll bet you'd be disappointed—not only because you didn't get to go to the game but because I let you down. If I do it once, you might forgive me, but if I keep making promises I don't keep, you will become so disappointed that you will stop trusting me or start resenting me.

Every married couple has expectations. Your grandmother expects me to remember her birthday, our wedding anniversary, Mother's Day, Valentine's Day, and a few other days I can't remember right now. (Shh! Don't tell her!) If I forget one of these days or remember too late to get a good present and end up picking up a bouquet of flowers from the supermarket on the way home, she will be disappointed. She doesn't clobber me or anything, but sometimes I know my thoughtlessness hurts and I always wish I had done better.

A relationship based solely on eros or phileo is absolutely destined to fail. No one can keep up their youthful good looks forever, and no one constantly meets the expectations of another. My point in all this is not to discourage you from getting married, but to help you understand the difference between these superficial types of love and the third and most wonderful love of all, *agape.*

Agape is another Greek word for love (those Greeks knew their stuff!). But it's in a league by itself. Agape is unlike anything we naturally know because it is the kind of love that God has for us. It really is a supernatural love.

Agape is totally unconditional—nothing on the part of another prompts it to be activated and nothing on the part of another can cause it to diminish or disappear. As I said, it's not natural. We tend to love people because they love us and are nice to us. We love people who are thoughtful, kind, shower us with nice gifts, and give generously without asking for anything in return. But if they are hateful, rude, selfish, and cruel, we tend to love them less. But that's not how God loves us, and it's not how He wants us to love each other. There is nothing we can do to make God love us more, and there is nothing we can do to make God love us less. He doesn't love us because we deserve His love or because we praise Him or because we are charitable. But even if we do something really terrible, He will never stop loving us.

Face it, guys. That is not the way you naturally feel about other people. If someone says hurtful things to you or tries to embarrass you in front of your friends, you probably don't feel a lot of love toward that person.

It's hard to even tolerate such people, much less like them, and certainly not love them.

That's why agape is so special—because it requires us to work at it. Unlike eros or phileo, agape doesn't just happen. No marriage ceremony can cause it to suddenly appear. There are no magic words or experience that will create a feeling of agape in you or in another. And no matter what, you will never completely master it. The longer and more diligently you practice it, however, the more natural it will become, but you'll be working on this for the rest of your lives.

The great myth of marriage is that you will start out as full of love as you can be. People think this because they tend to feel so happy on their wedding day, and elation quickly wears off as you realize that your husband snores or your wife leaves her hair in the shower drain. But remember: Love and happiness are not the same, and if you're doing things right, happiness may come and go depending on circumstances, but love will only get stronger and deeper.

I've said this before, but it bears repeating: You are not perfect, nor is your future spouse. And each of you is going to be imperfect in your own way. You might discover that one of you in the marriage is always punctual, the other habitually late; one will be very thrifty and never want to spend an unnecessary dime, the other almost reckless with money; one will think special occasions like birthdays are big deals that require elaborate celebrations, while the other thinks these are just regular days that at best should be acknowledged with a card; one of you will likely be very emotional, the other perhaps stoic to the point of seeming cold or unfeeling.

"But, Grandpa," you're probably thinking, "wouldn't it be easier to love someone who is similar to you—who believes what you believe and likes the same things you like?" I know it seems like that should be the case, but it isn't. Learning to love someone who is very different from you is how you grow. It's how you learn to be patient. It's how you learn to put others first. It's how you learn to make sacrifices for the sake of someone else. It's how you learn to try—and maybe even like—new things. It's what makes you a better person, and it's one of the reasons marriage is so great.

Being compatible with someone does not mean you have to be the same. If you stay with someone long enough and love them despite their flaws, you will become an extension of that person—finishing each other's sentences, anticipating each other's needs, knowing all of their favorite things. That, dear Chandler and Scarlett, is true compatibility. And blessed you are if you ever discover and experience it. But it probably won't happen on your wedding day.

The most perfect picture of real love I ever saw was in a most unlikely place. Back when I was a pastor in Texarkana, Arkansas, there was a retired minister from our church named Delbert Garrett, who had been married to his wife, Roberta ("Robbie"), for more than fifty years. Delbert and Robbie had spent their lives together, happily taking care of other people in our community through his pastoral ministry. After Delbert retired, Robbie was diagnosed with Alzheimer's disease, a horrible and slow-acting brain disorder that slowly takes away one's memory, personality, and eventually one's life. The symptoms first manifested themselves as Robbie started forgetting little things, like where she had placed her keys. Then she started forgetting bigger things, like when she had put food on the stove so she left it unattended and it completely burned up. Delbert kept an increasingly watchful eye on her so she wouldn't accidentally hurt herself or others.

One day, Delbert came home to find Robbie in the middle of the busy street in front of their home, where she was almost run over by traffic. Delbert realized he could no longer care for her at home, so he reluctantly found her a place in a long-term care center. Even though there were nurses to care for her twenty-four hours a day, Delbert insisted on feeding her each of her three daily meals himself. Several of us suggested that he let the nurses help, but he would have none of it. Faithfully and without complaint, he went to her bedside each and every day, seven days a week. As her condition worsened, she became increasingly unaware of her surroundings and forgot the names and faces of all her old friends and even family. Eventually, she no longer even recognized her loyal and faithful husband, but Delbert continued to stay by her bedside. Before long, even the long-term care facility couldn't attend to her needs, so she was moved to a local hospital where she would spend her final days.

One day I stopped by the hospital to visit Delbert. As I approached Robbie's room, the door was open and I heard Delbert talking, so I paused and peeked in. I'll never forget what I saw. Delbert stood by Robbie's bed with a dish in his hand, slowly and carefully feeding her spoonfuls of pureed food. All the while, he spoke gently to her: "Robbie, here's a little bit of potatoes. Come on, sweetheart . . . take just a bite . . . that's good, honey. Just swallow. That's it. Here's another bite, Robbie. That's good, sweetie."

With each patient touch of the spoon, he continued to say the kindest and most loving things to her, even though she was oblivious to all of it. She stared straight ahead at the wall, stuck in a catatonic state so deep that not only was she unable to recognize or respond to her husband, but she was able to swallow her food only thanks to her natural bodily reflexes.

It had been years since Delbert had known Robbie's kiss or even the conscious touch of her hand. He had not seen her smile or heard her call his name in almost a year. She was oblivious to the kind words or deeds he was performing on her behalf. He was giving her all he had and was receiving absolutely nothing in return. Not even a smile. It was as if she were dead, but as long as she had a heartbeat and a breath, Delbert loved her. He loved her not because he enjoyed it or found pleasure in it, but because fifty years earlier he had promised Robbie, God, and their closest friends and family that he would never leave her or forsake her until death parted them. And here he was, keeping that promise, faithful to the end.

As I watched this remarkable picture of true agape, I prayed to myself. "God, I wish every young lady in this world who is looking for love from some boy would one day know a love like this one. I pray that every man in this world would exhibit this level of commitment and love to the one he promised himself to."

Chandler, I pray that one day you will not just feel all giddy and emotional for a pretty girl or promise to be nice to her just because she is nice to you. I pray you will commit yourself absolutely to someone else and that you will be faithful and loyal and act lovingly toward her until one of you meets God in heaven.

Scarlett, I pray you never come across some boy who tries to use you or take from you without committing himself to you. (If that happens, come tell your grandpa or your daddy, and we'll take care of it.) I pray you find someone who loves you just as Delbert loved Robbie, and will remain at your side for the rest of your days.

There is a really great movie called *Forrest Gump* (and I hope you don't see it until you're *much* older), in which the title character, Forrest, says, "I am not a smart man, but I know what love is." I'm not that smart, either, but I know what love is. I saw it in a hospital hallway one day. I see it in your grandmother's faithfulness to me. And it's a love I hope you'll see all the days of your life.

CHAPTER NINE

On the Environment

Dear Chandler, Dear Scarlett:

Right now, you're probably too young to realize just how amazing nature is, and I worry that you'll end up like others in your generation who spend all their time inside playing video games or watching bad reality television. But if you're anything like your grandpa, you will spend a lot of your time outdoors—hunting, fishing, camping, hiking, and picnicking. You may decide you like to surf the mighty waves of the ocean or scale snowcapped mountains or simply tend a garden in your backyard, but I have no doubt you'll grow to appreciate the world around you.

I want you to grow up with a healthy, respectful love and appreciation for the earth and all the amazing things it offers. Of course, you should worship the Creator, not the created, but you will be in direct conflict with God Himself if you are careless with His most amazing invention. Every day, I am in awe of our magnificent and resilient planet, but I also know that, despite its sheer awesomeness, the earth is a very delicate place.

In the book of Genesis, God tells us that we "have dominion over" all of the things we see. That means we're supposed to utilize them for our benefit but also to manage and care for them as well. You have a lot of freedom to enjoy the truly amazing menu of natural resources on earth—the fruits, plants, and fish you can eat; the trees you can use to build homes and fires; the water for you to drink. But as with any great freedom, there comes great responsibility.

When I was eleven years old and in the Boy Scouts, I learned a valuable lesson: Always leave your campsite in as good or better shape than you found it. That's a pretty simple and straightforward rule, and even as an eleven-year-old boy I was able to understand it clear as day. Think about it: If someone let you borrow a favorite toy, would you destroy it before you gave it back to them? No—at least I hope not! You would take extra special care of it so they would stay your friend and trust you in the future if you ever wanted to borrow another one of their toys. The same is true for the planet. God has let you borrow it while you live, but it doesn't belong to you, and the people who live after you will have to deal with any mess you leave behind.

Despite how obvious this seems, most adults—be they Democrat or Republican, male or female, urban or rural—haven't managed to grasp this concept. Sadly, you are growing up in a time when the resources of our world have become ammunition in an unnecessarily bitter and divisive political battle in which people assume that our choice is either to destroy the planet and savage its every fish, plant, and animal or to become fanatics who protect lizards, rats, and twigs without any consideration for how these actions affect people. This doesn't even include the debate over global warming—something that even the top scientists in our nation haven't been able to agree on and that I will not try to explain right now. But regardless of whether you believe climate change is real, shouldn't we all agree that we have a responsibility to protect what God gave us? Wouldn't we fix a lot of our problems if we all followed the Boy Scout code?

Some people think I'm not a true "conservative" because of my commitment to protecting the environment. They forget that the root of the word "conservative" is "conserve." So who is more conservative than a conservationist? How can you call yourself a conservative if you don't think we should conserve the most precious resources we have available to us?

Just after I assumed the governorship of Arkansas in the summer of 1996, I had to decide whether or not to support a ballot initiative to amend the state constitution to designate an additional one-eighth of one penny in the state's sales tax for four agencies: the Game and Fish Commission, the Department of Parks and Tourism, the Department of Arkansas Heritage, and Keep Arkansas Beautiful. All of these agencies were responsible for protecting and preserving the state's abundant natural resources by rehabilitating our extensive state parks system and securing public lands so that the poorest kids in the state would be able to access areas for hunting, fishing, hiking, and camping without worrying that a handful of wealthy people would buy the property and restrict its use.

Because I was a conservative Republican who had

successfully fought tax increases in the past, people assumed I would oppose the amendment. But I hadn't opposed past increases simply because I am against tax increases; I opposed them because I knew whatever extra money the state brought in would be wasted. In this case, I thought the revenue would go toward a worthy cause. Though I would later pay a high political price for my position when I sought the Republican nomination for president in 2008, I shocked everyone when I told them that I not only supported it, but would personally travel the state to campaign for its passage. The measure, which had failed in previous attempts, passed by a majority of the Arkansas voters in November of 1996.

To this day, it remains one of the things I'm most proud of in my ten and a half years as governor. As I've explained, I grew up about as poor as most folks could have been in those days, and some of the only vacations and outings my family ever had involved fishing, camping, or hunting on public land that was available for anyone to use. In the summer, I would stay out of trouble by going to the local park, where I could swim and play on the playground. Arkansas is known for its natural resources and beauty—our state motto is "The Natural State"—with more than 9,700 miles of navigable rivers, 650,000 acres of freshwater lakes, beautiful mountains, grassy prairies, thick wooded forests, and vast wetlands that are home to the world's finest duck hunting. For those of us who love the outdoors, these are not things that should be taken for granted.

I knew that the amendment not only would benefit people like me, but, more important, would ensure that when the two of you grew up, you would be able to see the beauty of the state in the same way I had. I wanted you and every other kid in Arkansas to know the joys of catching a fish that you could clean and eat the same day. I wanted you to be able to watch a wild turkey strut and see a flock of mallards fly into flooded timberland. I wanted you to smell the aroma of fresh honeysuckle in the spring while walking through the woods, and to gasp at the unlimited view of the sky from the top of Mount Magazine's wonderful lodge. Plus, I'm convinced that real peace in life requires having a proper balance in your relationships with God, other people, yourself, and the world around you. I did not want to be the one responsible for throwing those relationships off balance!

As wonderful and as beautiful as Arkansas is, our world offers so many different types of landscapes that I hope you will be able to enjoy. When your grandmother and I were kids, we never dreamed we'd see the ocean. But a few years ago we decided to build a house on Florida's Gulf Coast so we could live on a beach and have the sea as our backyard. While we still have our house in Arkansas and always will keep roots there, we love living in Florida. Almost every day, I walk the beach at sunrise and find myself meditating on the vastness and the overwhelming beauty of what God has made.

When you come to visit your grandma and me, we'll walk that beach together, and you will look out at the Gulf of Mexico and see a seemingly endless expanse of the bluest water. You will hear the sounds of the waves crashing on the sugar-white sands of the shore and watch as dolphins play just beneath the surface of the sea. What you won't see is what lives under those vast waters—the thousands of species of plants and animals that survive as part of an intricate ecosystem in which each part plays a special role in sustaining life and the earth itself.

I confess, when I was a little kid, I took the natural world around me for granted. Grass was just a nuisance I had to mow; the pecan trees were irritating specimens that produced so many pecans that I spent many a backbreaking fall Saturday picking them all up. Back then I wished those trees would fall down. Now I'd love to have pecan trees in my yard and regret that I didn't appreciate them more when I was little.

I also didn't understand the essential value of wetlands, which are necessary in the South's low-lying areas because they serve as a natural filter and buffer for rainwater. Back then I only thought they were good for duck hunting. Then, one day in 2004, a flood devastated Franklin County in Arkansas. As I walked through the affected areas to inspect the damage to so many homes and local businesses, I saw how careless urban development had demolished those vital wetlands, thus literally paving the way for so many lives to be ruined by destroying the natural system that would have drained the rainwater.

We so often don't realize what things are worth until we lose them. I have some very old guitars that are real treasures to me. One of my favorites is a 1964 Gretsch Tennessean guitar that is identical to the one played by George Harrison of the Beatles in their famous 1964 concert in New York's Shea Stadium. Today this guitar is worth much more than it was back then because it's considered a true collector's item. When I was a teenager, I had a 1967 model that was just like it, but I was forced to sell it right before your uncle John Mark was born so your grandma and I would have enough money to feed his little face. It was very difficult to let go of my guitar, but I really didn't have a choice. I spent years looking for one just like it, and when I finally found someone who owned one, I gladly paid him many times over what I had sold mine for back in 1976.

There are some things we give up out of necessity, like I gave up those guitars. But there are some things we lose simply because we're careless. When I was nine years old, someone stole my bicycle because I'd left it in our yard without locking it up. The fact that I'd left the bicycle unlocked certainly didn't give the thief the right to take it, but if I had really valued my bicycle, I would have taken the steps to protect it before it was too late.

There are things you might look at and think they are just old and useless. Heck, you might look at me and think that! But if you see a tree that is 150 years old, you must understand that if something happens to that tree, there isn't a "tree store" where you can buy another one. Sure, other trees can be replanted and grown, but you will have to wait 150 years to get another one that is just as big and impressive.

A friend of mine whom you might meet and duck

hunt with someday is George Dunklin, Jr., of DeWitt, Arkansas. George might just be the most knowledge-able person alive when it comes to hardwood forest management. He owns thousands of acres of prime farm and timberland in south Arkansas, and could eas-ily chop down trees to sell for lumber or firewood and still have enough to last him for the rest of his life. But instead he diligently plants oak and other hardwood trees on his property to replace the ones he's cutting down. None of these trees will fully mature until long after he is gone, so why does he do it? Why does he spend money to plant trees that will cost him plenty but will not earn him a dime? Because he wants the genera-tions who come after him to know what a beautiful for-est looks like. He wants his descendants to be able to wake up on a cold winter morning before the sun rises, trudge through the cold snow, stand next to a beautiful oak tree as the sun starts to rise, and huddle quietly as they await the first flight of greenhead ducks breaking through the tops of the trees.

I hope you will do this as well and will stand in rev-erence at the majesty of God's creation when you hear the flutter of ducks' wings and the quacks as the ducks call out to one another. I hope you watch in awe as doz-ens of mallards begin to descend into the treetops, cup their wings ever so gracefully, and land so close to you that you can see the fog of their breath in the cold air. I hope you will love it as much as I do.

Luckily, you don't have to have the money to plant hundreds of oak trees in order to be a good steward of the environment. You can start now by doing things like throwing trash in a trash can instead of littering on the ground; recycling cans, bottles, and paper so they can be used again; turning off lights and electrical appliances when you're not using them; and walking on the sidewalk instead of the grass. These aren't big things, but doing these little things will make it easier for you to do the big ones later on. And if everyone did these little things, it could make a big difference.

There will be many people who will try to argue about the earth and make a political issue about how we take care of it. Leave them to their own small and sad worlds and spend your time appreciating the marvelous place where you live. The earth is your campsite. You don't own it. You just get to borrow it for a little while and then move on. Have a great time camping out, but pick up all the things you brought with you and don't take anything away but pictures. If you leave God's great campsite in as good or better shape than you found it, you will make your grandpa very proud.

CHAPTER TEN

On Creativity

Dear Chandler, Dear Scarlett:

By now I'm sure you know how much your grandpa enjoys music. I've probably sung or played guitar for you more than once, whether you were in the mood to hear me or not. But even if you don't enjoy my performances, I hope you have at least inherited my love of music.

I certainly won't insist you do something you don't enjoy doing, but somehow I think you'll play music at some point in your life. Even if you don't end up loving it, maybe you'll at least give it a try once you learn how much it drives your parents crazy! Part of growing up is finding ways to make your parents scream (your parents sure found ways to do it to me). And, trust me, a surefire way to do this is to practice music at home as loudly and as often as you can. You probably won't be very good at first, but that's even better. If you actually do try to improve, I promise to buy you an amplification system that will take sounds of even the quietest instrument to the decibel level of a four-engine jumbo jet.

Okay, the joy of music doesn't really come from making noise or driving your parents nuts—that's just an added bonus. It comes from discovering a talent that was hardwired into you long before you were born.

As the Creator of the Universe, God is not only the most powerful being ever, but the most creative one as well. And because you were made in His image, it stands to reason that He intended you to be creative, too. Of course, there are many ways to be creative and God is mysterious, so it's impossible to predict how your own creativity will manifest itself in you, but I hope you will spend your life trying to figure that out.

For me, creativity springs directly from music. I believe human beings are fundamentally musical creatures and that music is a powerful force, symbolically and emotionally. While you were still in your mother's womb, you were introduced to the sound and power of rhythm. No, I didn't play my guitar against your mothers' bellies. But the steady pulse of your heart created a beat all its own. To your parents and grandparents, the sound of your heartbeat was some of the most beautiful music they had ever heard because it let us know you were alive, healthy, and growing.

From the moment you arrived, people started singing to you. I sang to you and so did your grandmother, even though neither one of us would ever make the first cut on *American Idol*. We just couldn't help it. Singing is a natural phenomenon across the world, and even though people may come from different cultures, languages, and geographical regions, we all have our own music—it's a universal force that allows us to communicate, express emotion, and share our feelings with others in a poetic way.

Even though your parents were never invited to showcase their singing voices at Carnegie Hall, they intuitively sang to you from the day you were born. Sometimes they sang little songs to soothe you and make you sleepy, and sometimes they sang just to be funny when no one else was around or listening. You laughed some of your first laughs because your mother and dad sang songs you thought were funny. As you grow up, you'll sing, too. What comes out won't be recognizable as a song at first, but your grandpa will know you're just warming up for all the concerts you'll perform one day! As soon as you learn some real words, you'll start learning "real" songs, some of which will just be funny. But others will help you learn everything from colors to words to animals to lessons about right and wrong.

You'll also find other ways to express your creativity. You'll bang on things like pots and pans you pull out of the kitchen cabinets—because they *really* make some noise—or the tray on your high chair because you want to entertain yourself at mealtimes. Other people may think you're just getting accustomed to using your arms and hands, but I will think your inner drummer is starting to come out. If this is the case, I'm one step ahead of you—Grandpa already has a set a drums at his house just waiting for you to take your talent to a new level!

But music isn't the only natural creativity we share. You will most likely want to draw pictures from the first time your little hands can hold a crayon or pencil. My guess is that instead of limiting your efforts to a crayon on a piece of paper, you'll discover the joys of drawing with a permanent marker on the walls of your room.

Chandler, your dad really enjoyed using crayons, ballpoint pens, Magic Markers, and even your grandmother's lipstick to express himself on the Sheetrock walls of his childhood bedroom. If you could have seen all the gallons of paint your grandmother and I had to buy to cover up his mess, you'd probably think he was involved in a conspiracy with Sherwin-Williams. Judging by your father's persistence, I can only assume he was trying to re-create the frescoes of the Sistine Chapel in Rome on his walls. I've seen the Sistine Chapel, and, trust me, Michelangelo need not fear his place in art history will be supplanted by your father.

Scarlett, your mother was much more traditional in expressing her artistic side, opting for more conventional surfaces like paper. In fact, when your mother was barely four years old, she had her own "office" that doubled as a creative warehouse. It was located under my desk at the Beech Street Baptist Church back when I was pastor there. The preschool and kindergarten she attended for two years was at the church, so each day she came to work with me and hung out in my office until school started. To keep herself busy while I worked, she took paper, scissors, crayons, and paste, and hid under my desk as she set to work. While I was getting started on my day, she was busy pouring her little soul into making something special and original for her daddy. Over those few years, I built up quite the collection of pictures and some very interesting master-pieces she made for me under that desk.

Your uncle John Mark had his creative side, too, though he wasn't much for drawing. John Mark had and continues to possess a most vivid imagination. As a child he expressed this by using his toys as actors in his never-ending theater productions. He never simply played with his toy soldiers and action figures—he arranged them, staged them, and then directed them in his own version of a story that his audience (that would be me and your grandma) often didn't fully understand. But he loved it anyway. For a while, I worried that your uncle didn't get along well with your mom and dad, because he was perfectly happy being alone for hours with nothing but the "actors" and "sets" that he selected from his toy box to animate his own little world.

John Mark would go on to become a screenwriter for film, and looking back I should have realized that was inevitable. If talent plus sheer determination and desire amount to anything, he will win an Oscar someday. And when he thanks the "little people," I'll know he isn't talking to the grips, set designers, or camera operators, but to the little toy people that first inspired him.

Your own creative capacity will develop in many

ways. You will sing without being told to, draw pictures without being directed, and dance when you hear music that makes you want to move. You may not dance like the people you see at the ballet, but there isn't one right way to dance. You may just clap your hands, nod your head, move all around the room, or simply shake your leg while you sit. Unfortunately, I've never convinced your grandmother that my constant leg shaking is the uncontrollable need to dance. To her, it's simply annoying, and for more than thirty-eight years I've had to hear her say, "Stop shaking your leg! You're bouncing the table!" She even feels the shaking when we're sitting at a concrete picnic table, so I think she's just overly sensitive. I maintain that my uncanny knack for finding music to move to in all circumstances, at all times, and in all settings is not a nervous tic but a very natural expression of my energy and soul!

Your creative self will also naturally emerge as you do what your parents, grandparents, and every kid in the world does: act out characters. You may not star on Broadway or in feature-length films, but it will be impossible for you to play with your friends or toys without playing some sort of role. Even if we don't think of ourselves as actors, we all grow up with a natural propensity to playact. We imitate parents, teachers, people we see on TV, and even animals. It's as natural as breathing, and although most people just think of it as child's play, it's far more important than they give it credit for. Acting teaches us about how others feel and allows us to express our own emotions in a healthy, positive way. It also helps us exercise our imagination as we pretend to be something we're not, and this, in turn, makes our brain stronger.

When you play a role and make believe you are someone else, you are not just practicing for a future career in politics (though that skill certainly seems to come in handy for a lot of politicians these days). Whether you imagine yourself to be a doctor, a famous singer, or the president of the United States, you are learning how to think beyond yourself and use your imagination. And a good imagination is crucial if you want to be successful in life, because if you only do things the way they have been done before, you will never change the world. But if you learn to imagine, you will discover new ways to do old things, as well as ways to do things that have never been done before. And imagining yourself to be something you want to be is the first step to becoming it later on.

Chandler, your dad was quite the little actor as a child. He often mimicked what he saw me do, which was scary at times but provided me with some very funny memories. In his early years, when I was a pastor, David used to stand in the living room holding a Bible as big as he was, projecting his voice across the room and shouting something about God. I don't remember what he said—it changed every time—but I do remember that he never forgot to ask for the offering. He would grab one of his mother's bowls and pass it around the room hoping it would come back to him filled with dollars. I wasn't sure what he would go on to do in life, but I was pretty sure he would make money doing it. As David got older, he took his skills to a new level, performing in church musicals and high school plays, but his first stage will always be our living room.

Scarlett, your mother also liked to act, but did so in very different ways than your uncle. Sarah loved to pretend she was a homemaker and that her room was an apartment with its own little toy kitchen, a table and chairs for the elaborate imaginary meals she would serve, and a toy box filled with animals and little dolls that were her "guests." I was often the guest at the feasts and parties she would host in her room, and I have consumed enough imaginary food and tea to supply my caloric needs for a lifetime. Too bad I didn't consume more imaginary calories instead of taking on too many real ones!

Your mother also used her acting skills to avoid the levels of discipline that your uncles experienced. I've never known anyone who, when caught doing something wrong, could so convincingly display a degree of remorse that would make the Pope feel obliged to grant an indulgence. If Sarah misbehaved, she didn't run and hide like John Mark or stand and fight and defy authority like David. Rather, she would burst into tears, confess, and express the most profound sorrow and regret for having disappointed her daddy. More often than not, by the time she had cried enough tears to fill a bathtub, I was about ready to apologize to her! I probably did on a few occasions. A couple of times I was so reluctant to upset her any more than she already was that instead of giving her a spanking like her mother insisted, I would take her to her room, close the door, and then spank the bed instead of her. She, of course, would wail and cry as if she had been given the mother of all spankings, when in fact all she got was more acting experience. It was only later in life, long after I could punish her for past crimes, that the rest of the family found out what a soft touch I was for my baby girl and her tears. Good news for you: I still am.

As good as your parents were at acting, they never inherited your grandpa's love of music. Because I had played music since I was eleven years old, I always hoped my children would take a liking to it as well, but they were more interested in other things. John Mark played trumpet in the school band throughout high school, but his real interest was writing. Sarah tried piano for a while, but playing soccer and softball were much more appealing to her than playing scales for hours. In sports, she was her mother's daughter, being at age nine the first girl to ever play baseball on what had been an all-boys team in the city of Texarkana. What's more, she was actually better than most of the boys on the team.

At one point when David was a teenager, I thought he might be getting ready to discover a hidden musical gift within him. He decided that if his dad could play a guitar, how hard could it be? For Christmas when he was fifteen, he asked for a guitar, but since he was left-handed, we needed to get one that he could play (I'm right-handed, so none of mine would work). Left-handed guitars are more expensive than right-handed ones, but I was so thrilled that one of my sons might become a world-famous guitarist that money was no object (although at that time in our lives, it most certainly was!).

David received his left-handed guitar and, with it, the harsh reality that being a country star required more effort than simply picking up an instrument and walking onstage to the adulation of adoring fans. David didn't enjoy sitting all alone for hours, forcing his fingers to press against strings in what felt like torture just to play a simple chord. He hated practicing, but I think he really loved playing. Or maybe, he just loved playing *like* he was playing. In the end, though, he never wanted to spend the time to learn more than a chord or two and quickly abandoned music altogether. Then, after about a year, someone stole that guitar from David's dorm room at college. I was upset that I'd spent all that money on a nice guitar that wasn't really used and then was stolen, but hopefully the thief at least played it more than David did.

The ease with which you and everyone else express creativity proves music and art are essential to our growth as humans. I will do all I can to make sure you don't attend a school operated by the idiots who think music and art programs should be eliminated from the curriculum to save money for "more important" things. I know it's important for schools to teach math, history, and science as well, but I have never understood the sheer lunacy of educators who think having a football team is more important than having a marching band. Don't get me wrong—I love football. But I've never believed it makes me a smarter or more successful person. Having an outlet to exercise and explore your creativity, however, does.

Chandler and Scarlett, I don't know if you will be musicians, or artists, or dancers, or actors, or writers. Perhaps you won't be any of these things. But I know that you have a creative capacity within you—we all do. And if you develop it, you will be able not only to dream big things, but do big things. I'd love to go to your recitals and concerts someday and spend time watching videos of you playing music, acting in a school play, dancing in a ballet, reading stories you have written, or looking at your paintings and sketches. No matter what, please know that the arts—all of them—are a natural part of who you are. It may be that you like football more than the flute, or soccer more than Shakespeare, but you were made to connect with the creative part of you that God gave you. And if you also need help getting an instrument that is really loud so you can learn to play and drive your parents out of their minds, just know good ol' Grandpa is ready to help!

CHAPTER ELEVEN

On Pain

Dear Chandler, Dear Scarlett:

I need to make a confession to the both of you: Your grandpa is not exactly heroic when it comes to pain. Your grandmother's pain threshold is pretty high, and she can withstand a lot. Once she had to have both of her knees surgically replaced with titanium versions, and even though this is a very painful procedure and the doctor gave her the option of having one knee done at a time, she chose to have both done on the same day!

I could never do that. Sometimes I thank God I wasn't born a hundred years ago, when there were no painkillers or anesthetics and the only way people could deal with pain during surgery was to take a swig of whiskey, bite down on a stick, and scream until it was over. You'll know what I'm talking about if you ever see a John Wayne movie. But I am not John Wayne, and the real John Wayne is dead. I'm allergic to exactly two things: penicillin and pain. In my opinion, if God wanted me to suffer that much, He would never have invented class-A narcotics and anesthesia—or He would have at least made me like whiskey.

My aversion to pain probably goes back to my childhood trips to Dr. George Wright's office to get my vaccinations. I can still remember the gleaming eyes of his nurse Bertha Miller, who I swear took her job so she could torture little boys and seemed to get a sick pleasure out of stabbing what was probably a dull and rusty needle into my arm or my rear end. And to this day, I still break out in cold sweats at the memory of Dr. Sam Strong, my dentist, who once braced his knee on his dental chair so he could yank a tooth out of my mouth when I was all of five years old. Perhaps he forgot to give me Novocain, or maybe it just didn't work, but I can't even have my teeth cleaned without medication, and just thinking about Dr. Strong standing over me, grunting and scrunching up his face as he twisted and pulled, makes me want to run and hide the way I did when I was five. I'm not a bad patient when fully anesthetized into the stupor of deep sleep, but if I'm at all conscious, any ounce of courage I have disappears.

If I had my way, we would live in a world without pain. Unfortunately, that's not the world God made, and even if you've been lucky enough to inherit your grandmother's tolerance for pain, sometimes life is going to hurt.

You're probably already familiar with physical pain. It's unpleasant, but you'd better get used to it because you're going to have to live with it for your entire life. Some of it will be annoying but not terribly serious, like headaches, body aches, or a bad cough from a cold. Others might be more severe, like a broken arm or a bad cut you got because you weren't being careful. Scarlett, if you ever have a baby, you will suffer through the extraordinary pain of childbirth—another thing your grandmother was able to endure that would have made me faint! Hopefully, though, you'll forget how much it hurt as soon as you hold your son or daughter in your arms.

I pray you'll never experience the pain associated with a life-threatening injury like a car crash or bad fire. Even if you do, I trust you'll be brave and remember that not only is pain a blessing in disguise that tells us something is wrong with us, but God designed our bodies so perfectly that they can withstand immense injury and heal themselves with the right amount of care. Someone once said what doesn't kill us makes us stronger. That's true. Once you've lived through terrible pain, you're better prepared to deal with whatever else life throws your way.

Unfortunately, some of the most intense pain you will ever feel will not be the pain of your body, which tends to dissipate as you heal and can be tempered by medicine. This type of pain leaves no visible scars but can sometimes feel like a knife cutting through your heart. This is the pain your soul feels when you experience loss, disappointment, failure, or rejection. Like physical pain, there is no way to avoid it. But unlike physical pain, there are many ways to deal with and overcome emotional pain. And learning how to do so will mark the difference between living a life full of meaning and purpose or drifting away in a sea of self-pity and bitterness.

One of the biggest questions in the universe is "Why do bad things happen to good people?" There was even a bestselling book by Rabbi Harold Kushner that tried to answer this question, because it does seem a bit il-logical that bad things would end up befalling people who do good things. One would think that the only peo-ple who deserve a dose of disaster would be the really sleazy ones who steal from old people, make little girls cry, or hurt dogs. But some really horrible things hap-pen to some really nice people. What's worse is that some really good things happen to horrible people, and that might bug us even more!

A lot of people think bad things happen to us when we do something wrong. For example, if you say a bad word in the morning and then cut your finger while slic-ing tomatoes later in the day (which might prompt you to say another bad word), you might determine God is punishing you for your previous bad deed. This is how people explained suffering in the time of Job in the Old Testament. When Job was suffering from terrible ill-nesses and financial trouble, his neighbors speculated about what sin he must have committed to cause such a mess. To make matters worse, his friends abandoned him, so he had no one to help him through the pain. Later, when Jesus lived, His own followers asked Him what caused a seeing man to go blind—was it his own sin or the sin of his parents?

It's easy to dismiss such conclusions as old-fashioned.

You probably understand that people don't go blind because they did something wrong or that just because someone seems to have a lot of bad luck doesn't mean he's a bad person. But a lot of people still believe that if we're good we can avoid suffering, and if we're bad we'd better buckle up and brace for a major wallop. Unfortunately, it's not that simple.

Okay, it's true that in some cases our actions do lead us directly to suffer. When I was about four years old, I was playing with an old set of keys that I had found lying around my house. (You should feel sorry for me; I had so few toys as a child that an abandoned set of keys was more fun to play with than anything else I had!) I was having a perfectly fine time with the keys when, all of a sudden, I felt myself being thrown to the floor by the strong arm of my grandmother.

I was absolutely furious and so hurt that my own grandmother would purposely knock me to the floor. I didn't understand it at the time, but she wasn't angry with me for playing with the keys. In fact, she wasn't angry with me at all. Her sudden action was actually an act of love.

I later learned she had pushed me out of the way because I was putting the keys in an electrical socket. The holes in the socket looked about the same size as a key-hole, so this made perfect sense to me. My grandmother noticed what I was doing just as I had one key in the positive side of the socket and was about to insert another key in the negative side. My grandmother pushed me over because she knew something I didn't: that putting that second key in the other side of the electrical socket would have shocked and possibly killed me. She knew that whatever pain she inflicted on me by pushing me to the floor was nothing compared to the pain I would have experienced if she hadn't intervened.

I now understand that if I put metal in an electrical socket, I'm going to get shocked, and I hope you learn this lesson from reading this letter and not by trying it out on your own. There are plenty of ways people can bring pain upon themselves. If I drive over the speed limit or under the influence of alcohol, I run a greater risk of having a wreck. Likewise, if I eat too much, exercise too little, and fail to take care of myself, I really can't wonder why God would inflict me with diabetes or heart disease. If I started using drugs or drinking alcohol, I couldn't blame God if I lost my job, alienated my friends, and became sick. This is not rocket science, nor is it a mystery of the cosmos. I can't blame God for the outcome of my own conscious actions. It's as simple as that. Unfortunately, not all suffering is within our power to control.

Some suffering exists simply because we live in a broken world where human beings don't treat one another well. If someone steals from you or kills a loved one, that does not mean you did anything to deserve it. I wish I knew why people did such horrible things to others, but I'll let God judge them when the time comes. For the time being, comfort yourself with the fact that even if bad people go unpunished in this life, they will have to answer for their crimes in the next.

But what about the suffering that only God can control? What about debilitating diseases, like cancer, that inflict themselves on seemingly anyone—even children, who are innocent in God's eyes? What about natural disasters that wreak havoc and devastation on entire communities, not sparing the homes or lives of even the most honest residents?

I have lived through two tornadoes. The first happened when I was eleven years old and at home alone with my thirteen-year-old sister, Pat. I will never forget how, just before the storm hit, the sky outside turned extremely dark and everything seemed to grow silent.

It was difficult to breathe—as if all the oxygen had been sucked out of the atmosphere. And then, within seconds, all we could hear was the roar of the winds and the deafening crash of breaking glass and flying debris. I vividly remember seeing barrel-sized barbecue grills being tossed around our yard like paper airplanes. It scared the daylights out of both of us. We ran around trying to close doors and windows but kept being pushed to the floor by the winds. And even after the worst had passed, we still had to endure intense rain and hail. It was scary, but, fortunately, the damage to our house was minimal, and other than a few scrapes and bruises, Pat and I weren't seriously hurt.

The second tornado I lived through was much worse. Scarlett, your mother was just sixteen at the time, and she experienced it, too, so if she ever gets spooked by reports of a tornado or the sound of tornado sirens, please understand that she has good reason.

The tornado struck on January 21, 1999. Your grandmother was out of town, and I was having dinner about a block away from the governor's mansion. John Mark and David weren't living at home anymore, so your mother was home alone. All of a sudden I heard the sounds and felt that unforgettable sensation in the atmosphere that I remembered from when I was eleven. I knew a tornado was going to strike at any second, and I was right. Everyone at the dinner was herded into a basement as the twister roared overhead; minutes later, we all emerged to take stock of what had happened. Large trees that had stood for more than 150 years had been toppled over and the large Harvest Foods grocery store just across the street had been leveled. Two things went through my mind: One, as governor, I knew I would be responsible for organizing a search and rescue and marshaling the state's resources to aid in the recovery. Two, and even more important for the moment, I knew I needed to check on Sarah.

It was a nightmare to get back home, but luckily I had a state trooper escorting me. There was destruction everywhere—houses had been ripped from their foundations, and in the driving rain and darkness I could barely see twenty feet in front of me. The power had gone out, so we had to climb the electric gates to the grounds in order to get inside. Your mother was fine, though obviously shaken, but the property had suffered pretty much a direct hit. The mansion itself is virtually a fort and had little damage, but the nine acres of grounds around it were devastated, and smaller support structures used for equipment, maintenance, and storage were leveled. It was amazing to see how much damage could be done by something so natural as the weather.

We were lucky, though. Our family was safe and, as governor, I knew the property would be taken care of. But others in the community were less fortunate. Twenty-seven people were killed by that tornado and hundreds of others were injured. I didn't know any of these people personally, but I got to know many of their families in the aftermath as I toured the affected communities and talked with survivors. Most were still in shock over their sudden loss of loved ones, and many of them regretted not doing things that may have saved lives. It pained me to see how their suffering was made worse by the guilt they felt when, really, there was nothing they could have done.

I also found myself deeply moved by those who, despite losing pretty much everything they owned, expressed profound gratitude that they'd lived through it. On more than one occasion, a tornado survivor would say, "We lost everything, but all that stuff can be replaced. At least we're still alive." They focused on what they had left rather than what they had lost.

This is the key to dealing with the disasters in our lives. We need to avoid thinking of what we have lost and instead focus on what we have *not* lost. Knowing that life is more important than any material thing and understanding that God must still have a purpose for us if He spared our lives is the difference between coping with our pain and being debilitated by it.

As for victims of tornadoes, hurricanes, floods, or fires, I can't imagine they have all done something to "deserve" what they got. God may control the weather, but that doesn't mean storms only target bars and brothels and spare the churches. Even God-fearing people get clobbered, too.

Why is there suffering in the world? If God is all powerful, can't He rid the world of pain? Or at least save it as punishment for people who do bad things? Why does He punish good people and seem to reward the bad? What reasons could He possibly have?

I don't pretend to know why pain and suffering exist. I'm not God, and only He truly knows why He does what He does. But at the risk of being overly simplistic, let me try to help you understand.

In the book of Matthew, Jesus said that He "causes his sun to rise on the evil and the good, and sends rain on the righteous and the unrighteous." He does this not as a system of punishment and reward, but as a way to test our faith in Him. Think about it: It's easy to believe in God when everything is going right in your world or to shout "Praise God" when a tornado *misses* your house. The real test comes when you lose everything and still turn your faith and trust toward Him. It's like in sports. It's easy to root for a team when they're winning, but it's much harder to buy T-shirts and tune into every game if they lose all the time.

There was a man in our church in Pine Bluff by the name of Bill Garner. Bill was almost completely blind, had a prosthetic leg, and was severely disabled from the effects of diabetes. Yet Bill was one of the most cheerful and positive people I've ever known. If someone said, "Hi, Bill. How are you?" he always responded by saying, "I'm doing much better than I deserve," and he really meant it. Even though he had lost his sight, his mobility, and part of his hearing, he never had an unkind word for anyone or anything. It would have been easy and even understandable had Bill become reclusive and bitter for the situation he was in. But not only did he show up at church for every service, he was the most faithful volunteer we had. He made hundreds of phone calls every week to invite people to church, check on the sick, and encourage people who were dealing with something difficult in their lives. What he couldn't do with his legs and his eyes he did with what he had left: his fingers, his voice, and his loving spirit. Bill Garner suffered every day of his life, but instead of focusing on what he had lost, he made the most of everything he still had. His suffering didn't stop him—it just helped him appreciate all the joy in his life even more.

Sometimes God allows us to suffer in order to help other people. Your great-grandfather (my father) was a firefighter. His job was to go into houses that were on fire to try to get people out of them safely. Every time he did that, he risked getting killed himself, but he knew if he didn't go in, someone else might perish. He was never seriously hurt, but often suffered injuries, like a sprained ankle, pulled muscle, or scorched lungs from breathing in too much smoke. He was lucky. Plenty of firefighters die every day doing the same things he did, but instead of mourning the loss of his friends or quitting because he was too scared for his own life, he went to work every day knowing what good he was doing in the world and that God had put him on this earth to help people. He was fully prepared to die doing it because that was his duty: to save someone else's life.

Like firefighters, soldiers in our military often suffer terrible injuries and traumas, and some of them die to protect the lives of innocent people in war. Even peaceful missionaries and aid workers are sometimes murdered trying to get food, water, and clothing to people who lack these basic necessities of life. And even if they don't suffer physical pain, many of them suffer emotional pain as they watch terrible things happen around them. Even if we don't purposefully put ourselves in harm's way, we can never know how our suffering will change someone else's life—or even our own lives—for the better.

One of the most traumatic—and yet most natural—things in life is death. Will Rogers, an American humorist who lived and died long before your time, once observed that there are only two things in life that are certain: death and taxes. Because a lot of people (not your grandpa!) have figured out how to avoid paying taxes, the only thing that is guaranteed in life is that we will die at some point.

I don't expect you to really understand death right now. Fact is, I don't understand too much about it myself even though I've dealt with it more than I wish I had. I could try to give you a lot of deep theological and philosophical explanations for death, but all you really need to know is that nothing lasts forever. From the moment we are born, we are on borrowed time and have to accept that this life will eventually end. But even though this is something we all have to face—no matter how good or bad we are—that doesn't mean it's easy to cope with or understand.

I suppose one reason God invented death is that it makes life more precious. We tend to truly value the things that we can lose. That's why people walk around in an unfamiliar city with their hands clutching their wallets or purses—because they fear someone might steal their hard-earned money. But you never see people with their hands down their throats trying to hang on to their gallbladders. That's because it would be pretty difficult to steal someone's gallbladder. If we didn't have to worry about dying, there would be no reason to appreciate life, because we wouldn't worry about losing it.

The reason death is so painful to deal with is because we really don't know what happens to us afterward, and we have to rely on our faith to tell us that death is not the end, but just a transition.

In the years I served as a pastor, I saw death up close,

presiding over several hundred funeral services, and being present on many occasions when someone breathed his last breath and passed into eternity. One thing I learned was that people who believed that there was life beyond this one tended to deal with their grief more calmly, knowing they would eventually be reunited with their loved ones in heaven. Nonbelievers had a much harder time, crying uncontrollably at the thought of never seeing someone again. It was much harder to console these people. There was an audible difference in the very sound of their crying, which rang with an emptiness that was chilling. It was a sound I'll never forget.

Chandler and Scarlett, I want you to live longer, healthier, and more fulfilled lives than any of those who have gone before you. As long as I'm around, I will do everything I can to make sure that happens. But I can't protect you from having to face all the pains you'll face or the hurts you'll have or the blunt force that you will feel when someone close to you dies. It may be one of your pets, one of your relatives, or even a friend. It will happen and it will hurt. But I hope that when it happens you won't despair but take comfort in the fact that your life was better for having known that person and, if you put your trust in God, you will be reunited one day.

Losing someone is one of the most painful things you will ever have to endure. But a lonely, loveless life cuts much deeper into your soul than any heartbreak ever will. The deeper the love and greater the bond and relationship you have with someone, the more it will hurt when they leave. That's okay. You will learn to deal with that pain. What you can't deal with is a life without love, without the pure, boundless joy that comes from pouring your heart into someone else. So as much as I pray that you will live a life without much pain, I pray even harder that you will love and know many people. That you will do things to make the world a better place, even if they might hurt sometimes.

I hope to be around for as much of your lives as possible. I want to see your first music recital and your first soccer game. I want to be there when you get dressed for the senior prom and when you walk across the stage to get your high school diploma. I want to be there to watch your parents cry in sadness when they pack you up for college and be there to watch them cry in joy when you graduate from college and are finally on someone else's payroll besides theirs. I want to be there on your wedding day when you walk down the aisle of a church and pledge your life to another human being.

And I want to be there on the day you hold your own child in your arms for the first time. The greatest thrill you will ever know is the one you experience when you caress for the first time a child who is the very fruit of your own life. And if science catches up quickly enough, maybe I'll even be there when you experience the joy of holding your first grandchildren—the same joy I felt the first time I held each of you.

Chandler and Scarlett, as much as I want to be there for all those moments, I probably won't make it to all of them. I'm already on the back side of the journey, and I have to face the reality that one day God will call me home. When that happens, I hope I get the chance to tell you one last time how much I love you and how proud I am of you. I hope you will know how much joy getting to know you and hold you and watch you grow has brought into my life. I hope you remember me fondly and that all my faults and failures die with me, leaving you to take our family heritage to a new level of honor, integrity, and Godliness.

When that day comes, I'll be sad to leave and to know how much of your lives and your children's lives I'm going to miss. But don't think I'm gone forever! I'll be looking down on you from heaven, waiting for the day when you can join me.

Dear Chandler, Dear Scarlett

I wrote these letters so that long after I'm gone, you'll know that I loved you, had great hopes for you, and wanted to give you my best advice on living in this tough world. If I can't be there with you, I hope my letters and the lessons from them will act as a sort of reminder of me—as if I'm standing there beside you, whispering in your ear, and putting my arm around your shoulder. But most of all I hope these letters show you how much I love you—now and always.

Love,

Grandpa

Acknowledgments

As an author my relationship to a book is ever changing. When I first conceive of it and present it to my publisher, I love it. When I'm under the pressure of writing and hitting all the deadlines, I am challenged by it. And though it's sometimes tedious, there is a certain satisfaction in putting a chapter to bed. When I send the final chapter to be reviewed by the copy editors, I feel sheer elation. When I wade through grammatical marks and answer what seem to be endless queries (those pesky editor questions to "Name the person you discuss on page fifty-four" or "What color was the sweater she was wearing?"), I come to hate the book and want it to be over like a root canal! Then a

185

few weeks later, I get the galley proof and sit and read it without the marks and queries. Then I get to read it as you will and decide, does it make me laugh? Does it make me cry? Does it teach me something worthwhile? Does it entertain as well as educate? In other words, do I like it again?

This was a fun book to write but also therapeutic. And you know what? I like it. I really hope you do as well.

I owe much to the team at Penguin who has continued to believe in me and with whom I've had the joy of producing several consecutive *New York Times* bestsellers. Adrian Zackheim is the publisher and team leader who ultimately says "yes" to a project. Will Weisser, Brooke Carey, Julia Batavia, Allison McLean, and Margot Stamas are involved in editing, production, promotion, and distribution. Frank Breeden, my literary agent from Premiere Authors, has helped build a strong relationship with my publisher, which makes the entire process a pleasure; and Duane Ward and his team from Premiere Marketing put together a schedule for book signings that would make a presidential campaign look like a vacation.

And my biggest thanks is to you, the reader, who had

faith that the purchase of this book would be worth your time and your money. I've done my best to make it worth both. If you agree, tell everyone you know. If you don't, then please just keep that between us!

With heartfelt gratitude,

Mike Huckabee